A Journal of the American Civil War

EDITORS:

Theodore P. Savas and David A. Woodbury

VOLUME FOUR   NUMBER FOUR

Published quarterly by Regimental Studies, Inc., a nonprofit charitable corporation

---

STATEMENT OF PURPOSE: Regimental Studies, Inc., is a non-partisan, non-profit charitable corporation founded to further two specific goals. First, it is hoped that Civil War Regiments will encourage further research into the often neglected area of unit history studies by providing a serial outlet for that research. It is also our intent to raise funds for the preservation and protection of endangered Civil War sites by donating proceeds to various preservation organizations. To this end, your active support in the form of donations, advertisements, articles, and subscriptions, is both encouraged and welcomed. Thank you.

Subscription and General Information

Civil War Regiments is published quarterly by Regimental Studies, Inc., a nonprofit charitable corporation located at 1475 South Bascom Avenue, Suite 204, Campbell, CA 95008. Editors: Theodore P. Savas and David A. Woodbury. Voice: (408) 879-9073. Facsimile: 408-879-9327.

Trade distribution is handled by Stackpole Books, 5067 Ritter Road, Mechanicsburg, PA 17055-6921. 1-717-796-0411 (phone); 1-717-976-0412 (fax). Dealer inquires welcome.

SUBSCRIPTIONS: $27.00/year, ppd (four books), individual and institutional. Most individual issues may be ordered at $8.00 each. ppd., except for special theme issues, which are individually priced. Write to Back Issues, *CWR*, 1475 South Bascom, Suite 204, Campbell, CA 95008, or call 1-800-848-6585, for pricing information and availability. Please specify the volume and issue number when placing your order. Prepayment with check, money order, or MC/V is required. Two hundred and fifty signed and numbered four-issue Collector's Sets for the premier volume were printed. Cost is $40.00 ppd. Inquire as to availability. FOREIGN ORDERS: Individual issues are $10.00 each, ppd., and subscriptions (four issues) are $35.00/year, ppd. Payment in United States currency only or MC/V. Books shipped surface mail. Allow eight to twelve weeks for delivery.

MANUSCRIPTS AND CORRESPONDENCE: We welcome manuscript inquiries. For author's guidelines, send a self-addressed, double-stamped business envelope to: CWR-Editor, 1475 South Bascom, Suite 204, Campbell, CA 95008. Include a brief description of your proposed topic and the sources to be utilized. No unsolicited submissions will be returned without proper postage. Book review inquiries or submissions should be directed to Dr. Archie McDonald, Book Review Editor, Stephen F. Austin University, Department of History, P.O. Box 6223, SFA Station, Nacogdoches, Texas 75962-6223. (409) 568-2407. Enclose a self-addressed-stamped-envelope if requesting a reply.

This journal is printed on 50-lb. J.B. Offset recycled, acid-free paper

Thanks to your support, *Civil War Regiments* has been able to make a number of donations to Civil War-related preservation organizations. The recipients of these donations are listed below:

(LIFE MEMBER) ASSOCIATION FOR THE PRESERVATION OF CIVIL WAR SITES

RICHARD B. GARNETT MEMORIAL , HOLLYWOOD CEMETERY

HERITAGEPAC / CIVIL WAR ROUND TABLE ASSOCIATES

SAVE HISTORIC ANTIETAM FOUNDATION / TURNER ASHBY HOUSE, PORT REPUBLIC, VA

THE COKER HOUSE RESTORATION PROJECT, JACKSON, MS CWRT

AMERICAN BLUE & GRAY ASSOCIATION

APCWS 1993 MALVERN HILL/GLENDALE CAMPAIGN

Civil War Regiments, Vol. IV, No. 4, Copyright 1995

by Regimental Studies, Inc.

ISBN 1-882810-11-2

CONTRIBUTORS:

Frank A. O'Reilly graduated in 1987 with a B.A. in American History from Washington and Lee University and accepted a full-time position as historian at the "Stonewall" Jackson Shrine in 1990. In addition to numerous articles on the Civil War, O'Reilly is the author of *Stonewall Jackson at Fredericksburg* (Lynchburg, 1994), and the co-author of *The Atlas of the Civil War,* edited by James M. McPherson. He is currently working on a book on the Chancellorsville Campaign.

David L. Preston graduated *magna cum laude* from Mary Washington College in Fredericksburg with a B.A. in history in 1994, and is currently pursuing graduate studies in early American History at the College of William and Mary. He has worked as both a seasonal and an intern for the Fredericksburg and Spotsylvania National Military Park.

Kevin E. O'Brien is a Clerk of Court for the U.S. Bankruptcy Court in the District of Arizona. His received his B.A. and M.A. from the University of Pennsylvania and his J.D. from American University. He has written a number of articles on the Civil War, and is currently editing the previously unpublished memoirs of William McCarter for publication by Savas Woodbury in late 1996.

Gregory A. Mertz is a historian at the Fredericksburg-Spotsylvania National Military Park. He has written a number of Civil War articles, including a recent "General's Tour" on the Battle of the Wilderness for *Blue & Gray Magazine.*

Richard F. Miller / Robert F. Mooney co-authored *The Civil War: The Nantucket Experience* (Wesco, 1995). Miller, a graduate of Harvard and Case Western Reserve University Law School, is currently cataloguing the MOLLUS Collection at the Houghton Library at Harvard. He has a forthcoming article in Volume Five of *Civil War Regiments* entitled ". . .And Johnny Came Marching Home: The 45th Massachusetts Volunteer Regiment." Co-author Robert Mooney, who graduated from Holy Cross and Harvard Law School, has written extensively on Nantucket, and is the author of *The Advent of Douglass* (Wesco, 1991), and *Tales of Nantucket* (Wesco, 1992).

A Journal of the American Civil War

The Battle of Fredericksburg

continued. . .

Table of Contents, continued

The Confederacy's ". . .easiest major triumph of the war."

The Battle of Fredericksburg Revisited

_____

Theodore P. Savas

One prominent historian of the Army of Northern Virginia, while writing of that army's military campaigns, concluded that the Battle of Fredericksburg "must be reckoned its easiest major triumph of the war." Few would argue with Robert K. Krick's assertion. The ease with which this "major triumph" was earned, however, may well account for the unusually scarce number of secondary accounts written about the campaign. Comparatively speaking, the fighting at Fredericksburg has been virtually ignored for over thirteen decades.

To many, Fredericksburg lacks the compelling drama of a Chancellorsville (capped as it was with the mortal wounding of the irreplacable Thomas J. "Stonewall" Jackson), the climactic overtures of a Gettysburg, or the sheer intensity of a bloodletting like Spotsyvania Court House. Yet, those that ignore this engagement are and have been cheating themselves, for the cast of characters on both sides, coupled with the fascinating chain of events that unfolded west and south of one of America's most historic cities, makes for compelling reading.

This collection of six articles, while not intended as a definitive account of the battle, offers enthusiasts of the Civil War an opportunity to read and learn of several major events, units, personalities, and actions that helped shape the course and outcome of the fighting. Rather than offer articles covering well-known events in cursory fashion—a style much in vogue these days—these essays delve deep into specific slices of the battle that have been generally ignored or glossed over in popular accounts.

For example, most students of the war know that Confederate Brig. Gen. Thomas Cobb was mortally wounded while defending what would become a famous stone wall on Marye's Heights. Yet, how many are aware that a persistent controversy exists over how he was wounded (artillery or rifle fire), where he was wounded, and when he was struck down? William and Mary graduate student David Preston carefully peels back the layers of contradictory evidence that envelop this event and confidently assesses these disputes as he "solves" each mini-mystery enshrouding the death of that promising Georgia general. Still fewer students are aware that a vicious and bloody street fight took place two days before the main event of December 13, when the 20th Massachusetts Infantry drove through the streets of Fredericksburg in an attempt to clear out the pesky (and deadly) Confederates holding the bombed-out buildings and alleyways. Relying primarily on contemporary letters and journals of several of the participants, writers Richard Miller and Robert Mooney describe in detail how the engagement came about, where and how it was fought, and its impact on the participants.

These are but two of the five examples of the "slices" of Fredericksburg battle history contained in this collection. In keeping with our commitment to increase the usefulness of our articles, each is enhanced by the custom maps of North Carolina cartographer Mark A. Moore, who graciously agreed to donate his time and energy to *Civil War Regiments*. We are both lucky and thankful to have him.

Below is a deliberately concise account of the Fredericksburg Campaign, keyed to the various articles in this collection.

The Fredericksburg Campaign: A Synopsis

Following Robert E. Lee's Maryland Campaign of September 1862, Maj. Gen. Ambrose E. Burnside was appointed on November 7 to replace George B. McClellan as commander of the Federal Army of the Potomac. Burnside almost immediately decided on a plan that called for moving his army southeast to Fredericksburg so as to interpose his troops between Lee's Army of Northern Virginia and the Confederate capital at Richmond. Such a move, if successful, would provide several strategic and tactical advantages to the Federals. Burnside, with his army now organized into three large segments impressively dubbed "Grand Divisions," moved down the left bank of the Rappahannock River as Lee's scattered divisions began coalescing on the opposite side of that stream.

But as so often happens in war, matters did not progress exactly as intended. Burnside's senior commander, Maj. Gen. Edwin V. Sumner, reached Fredericksburg with his Grand Division on November 17. Although he faced virtually no organized opposition, Sumner loitered for two days too long (the river was easily fordable in at least one location), and by the 19th large portions of Lee's army had arrived on scene. Sumner's lethargic movements, coupled with a logistical snafu that caused an inordinate delay in the arrival of a pontoon train that Burnside was relying upon to cross the river, did not bode well for the Federals.

Arguing that Fredericksburg proper was useful to Lee's Confederates, Burnside opened a massive artillery bombardment on December 11, while ordering pontoon bridges constructed in three places over the wide river to facilitate the crossing of his army. Although the span constructed well south of Fredericksburg was erected with little difficulty, Federal engineers encountered stout and deadly opposition at the two proposed bridge sites in town. In a defense that has garnered well-deserved accolades, Brig. Gen. William Barksdale and his Mississippians stubbornly defended the town's riverfront until boat loads of Federal infantry crossed the Rappahannock and drove them into and beyond the town. (*Across the River and into the Streets: The 20th Massachusetts Infantry and the Fight for thr Streets of Fredericksburg*, by Richard F. Miller and Robert F. Mooney.) December 12 was an uncomfortable day for the Confederates, who witnessed senseless acts of wanton destruction in and about the historic city. Anger and revenge became powerful motivators.

As Burnside marshalled his forces (about 115,000 men) on the right bank of the river, Lee's army (about 78,000 men) was solidly deployed in a line some seven miles long. His left flank, held by Lt. Gen. James Longtreet's First Corps, lined the commanding terrain that towered over the open plain immediately west of the city, while the right portion of his army, Lt. Gen. Thomas J. "Stonewall" Jackson's Second Corps, lay thickly deployed on the undulating ground to the south and west of Fredericksburg. Because of a deep re-entrant angle in the center of Lee's line (meaning that the line bulged in towards the Confederates and away from the Federals), the only possibility for a successful assault— though the likelihood of such an event was virtually nil—was against either end of the meandering Southern line. Thus Burnside determined to launch his primary assault against Jackson's front, with a second diversionary attack against Longstreet and the heights behind Fredericksburg. Muddled orders from Burnside, however, coupled with an unusual set of circumstances, caused this plan to go fatally awry.

The long-awaited offensive finally got underway on December 13 when Maj. Gen. William Franklin's three divisions moved out in search of Jackson. An incredible exhibition of the use of artillery by John Pelham, who had taken up a position with a lone cannon that enfiladed the Federal line, turned what was essentially a simple forward movement into a chaotic affair. Pelham's artillery ultimately halted and ultimately weakened the attacking force, while concurrently boosting Southern morale.

When the Federals finally moved out in earnest, Confederate artillery on and around Prospect Hill, a commanding piece of ground near the right flank of Jackson's line, devastated the attackers (*"A Severe Day on the Artillery": Stonewall Jackson's Artillerists and the Defense of the Confederate Right*, by Gregory Mertz.) With the support of counter-battery fire, Franklin's men eventually reached a 600-yard gap inadvertently left in Jackson's front line. A division of veteran Pennsylvanians managed to pour through the breach. While the matter appeared serious for a short while, the depth of Jackson's front and the lack of any substantial Federal support did not leave the matter in doubt for long, and the attackers stumbled in retreat after suffering severe casualties (*"Busted up and Gone to Hell": The Attack of the Pennsylvania Reserves at Fredericksburg*, by Frank O'Reilly.)

Meanwhile, Longstreet's wing of the Army of Northern Virginia was methodically slaughtering line after line of Federals as they poured out of Fredericksburg to assault the impregnable Marye's Heights one-half mile west of the city (*"The Breath of Hell's Door": Private William McCarter and the Irish Brigade in the Attack on Marye's Heights: An Unpublished Memoir*, edited by Kevin E. O'Brien.) The ridge was scarred with a several hundred yard stretch of sunken road near its base that was lined with a stone retaining wall facing the city. The position was tailor-made for defense, and Thomas Cobb's Georgians, among others, utilized the position to good effect (*"The Glorious Light Went Out Forever": The Death of Brigadier General Thomas R. R. Cobb*, by David Preston.) Employing outmoded tactics that would be reprised hundreds of times during the First World War, Northern soldiers lined up and charged repeatedly across the open plains, where they were shot down by the thousands. Not a one reached the Confederate position. Casualties ran approximately eight-to-one on this portion of the field.

Although Burnside considered attacking again the next day, several of his officers managed to talk him out of such foolishness. The Army of the Potomac re-crossed the pontoon spans on the evening of December 15-16, 1862, and the battle that few historians have deemed worthy of study came to an end. Union casualties were approximately 13,000, while Confederate losses totalled less than 5,000. The Confederate army's lopsided victory must indeed, as Robert Krick has written, ". . .be reckoned its easiest major triumph of the war."

Introduction

William Marvel

It was many years before Ted Turner conceived of *Gettysburg*, or before I ever took an interest in Ambrose Burnside, that I first speculated what a poignant and spectacular movie could be produced around the Battle of Fredericksburg. The personality conflicts and uncertainties at Federal headquarters, the air of someone-has-blundered tragedy on the Union right, and the desperate courage and pathos on Marye's Heights offer the dramatic elements that ought to have inspired a worthy screenwriter by now. The saga of the bridges, the barrage of the city, the street fighting, and John Pelham's valiant foray would yield more heroic vignettes than anyone might expect from fiction. In one film, a director might combine the best of *Patton*, *The Charge of the Light Brigade*, and *Gallipoli*. But, thus far no one has taken the bait.

Fredericksburg does, however, seem to be earning its deserved scholarly attention at last. Three generations have been subjected to Edward Stackpole's slanted and uncritical *Drama on the Rappahannock* (Harrisburg, 1957), as well as his 1965 National Park Service publication on the battle. It is doubly unfortunate that the availability of those two sources has both crystallized the public image of that battle and discouraged more careful study of it, but at least the latter half of that misfortune seems to have come to an end. Serious examinations of Fredericksburg's various segments have surfaced during the past decade, and a comprehensive, professional analysis can be expected in the next few years from a Midwestern scholar.

The essays in this issue of *Civil War Regiments* form a part of that new scholarship. After a century and a third, researchers are finally willing to dig deeper into contemporary sources and reevaluate the tragedy of Fredericksburg without all the jaundice of earlier, simpler, and more convenient judgments. Twenty years ago, what historian would have adopted Burnside's assertion—as historian Greg Mertz does in his piece on Confederate artillery—that he actually intended William Franklin's assault against the Confederate right to be the principal attack? In the shadow of Stackpole's accepted malediction, the prevailing opinion has painted that intention as nothing more than Burnside's ex-post facto excuse, with which he hoped to shift the blame to Franklin. Stackpole would have us believe that Burnside abandoned that strategy before the fight, or sent Franklin vague orders in an effort to prepare him as a scapegoat against the possibility of defeat. Similarly, Mertz alludes to the rising pitch of battle on the Union left as the evidence Burnside needed to launch Edwin Sumner's attack against Marye's Heights. Stackpole, however, has broadcast the myth that Burnside sent in Sumner'assault in desperation after he supposed Franklin's movement had failed. These incidental references bespeak a subtle historiographical shift.

In addition to Mertz's examination of the role played by Stonewall Jackson's artillery, this issue includes a close look at the killing of Confederate Brig. Gen. Thomas R. R. Cobb, the assault of the Pennsylvania Reserves on Stonewall Jackson's front, the 20th Massachusetts Infantry and the Rappahannock River crossing and subsequent fight in the streets of the city, and an unpublished memoir by a member of the Irish Brigade detailing the attack on Marye's Heights. Here is the battle dissected into some of its parts, with each segment closely investigated. Most of these selections are based to some extent on previously unknown or little-known contemporary manuscripts, and like all new scholarship, its value increases with the proportion of material that is drawn from such sources. Once the parts have been reviewed and reassembled, the events of December 13, 1862, will emerge a little more distinctly from the fog of war.

Of course, much remains to be learned about this battle, from the psychology at headquarters to the motives behind the city's pillage. And then there are the details of human interest: for instance, did Joshua Chamberlain really sleep behind a breastwork of bodies the night after the battle, or did the 20th Maine withdraw to bivouac beyond the nearest casualties, as Chamberlain's major insisted years afterward? The answers to such tempting tales may diminish Fredericksburg's stock as a screen possibility, but no one seems to be snapping up that idea anyway.

The Assault of the Pennsylvania Reserves at Fredericksburg

Frank A. O'Reilly

Edward W. Steffen of the 121st Pennsylvania Volunteers wrote "I once had an idea that they were making good progress, but that idea has since faded away entirely." Speaking of the Federal government in the winter of 1862, he concluded, "They are now only slaughtering men for mere amusement it would seem. All those who participated in the Fredericksburg battle will testify to this."[1] Steffen spoke with the bitterness of many of the Federal soldiers who survived the Battle of Fredericksburg, but particularly for the broken remnants of the once strong Pennsylvania Reserves. The division had courted victory and disaster in the killing fields of Fredericksburg; and they traced their demise back to the opening week of November 1862.

On November 7, Maj. Gen. Ambrose E. Burnside superseded the Army of the Potomac's charismatic leader, Major General George B. McClellan. When news spread, the men were devastated. Charles H. Veil of the 9th Reserves reminisced that "many shed tears." Evan M. Woodward, adjutant of the 2nd Reserves remembered the outpouring of emotion at McClellan's final review, writing, "His departure from the army was a scene never to be forgotten." Another wrote, "We thought a great mistake had been made by the authorities."[2]

Burnside never replaced McClellan in the affection of the army. One of the Pennsylvania Reserves admitted "This division generally has a good opinion of Burnside," but most longed for McClellan's return. Edward Steffen hoped "that the troops will fight as good under Burnside as they ever did under McClellan."[3]

The Pennsylvania Reserves more than made up for its uncertainty for Burnside with a strong confidence in its own fighting ability that transcended any change in command. The division had thirteen veteran regiments that tasted battle in the Shenandoah Valley, the Seven Days battles around Richmond, Second Manassas, and the Maryland Campaign. It had entered the ranks of the Army of the Potomac with 10,000 men and one year later it had less than 4,000 left. Two newly raised regiments, the 121st and 142nd Pennsylvania Volunteers, brought the division's strength up to nearly 4,500 men. They believed in their commanders. Major General John F. Reynolds had led the division and now commanded the Federal First Corps. The division's new head was the no-nonsense professional, Brigadier General George Gordon Meade. Meade was an ugly and dour man, with a notorious hair-trigger temper. A close friend of Meade's observed that the general had "a tremendous temper, a great idea of military duty, and is very particular. When he does get wrathy, he sets his teeth and lets go a torrent of adjectives that must rather astonish those not used to little outbursts." Yet he managed to balance the difficulty of being Reynolds' constant rival and closest friend. The officers and men of the division knew nothing but respect for Meade.[4]

General Burnside went to work quickly. He grouped the various army corps together into "Grand Divisions." The Pennsylvania Reserves found their First Corps coupled with the Sixth Corps to form the Left Grand Division under Major General William B. Franklin, a bland, unimaginative disciple of McClellan. On November 15, the van of Burnside's army slipped out of Warrenton and headed east toward Fredericksburg. The Pennsylvania Reserves broke camp the next day, marching through Fayetteville, Morrisville, Hartwood, to Stafford Court House. The troops hiked for two days across fields paralleling highways crammed with artillery and wagons. Arriving at Stafford Court House, the Pennsylvanians discovered Federal cavalry housed in the public buildings and county records strewn carelessly about the streets.[5]

Burnside's army massed along the Rappahannock River opposite Fredericksburg. With no means to cross the rising river and the Confederates daily growing stronger, the Union commander paused to think out his next move. Meade's division moved south to Brooks Station on the Richmond, Fredericksburg, and Potomac Railroad. Establishing a camp in a pine thicket on November 22, the soldiers passed the time building shelters and repairing roads. The weather turned cold and snowy and supplies became scarce.[6]

George G. Meade struggled to maintain discipline in his division when supplies failed to get through. Christening their camp "Starvation Hollow," the

Reserves felt free to state their needs by any means at hand. Franklin Boyts related that the area was "not safe for chickens, hogs, or sheep to be about." Members of the 13th Pennsylvania Reserves waged a personal war to alleviate their hunger. Known as the Pennsylvania Bucktails, these adept hunters ravaged the country, carrying off everything from sheep to fence rails. Even when one captain tried to curb the Bucktails' ardor, the soldiers "broke loose before his very eyes" and stole every fence in the neighborhood. Meade tried vainly to stop their transgressions. The general personally broke up several marauding parties and even cornered an officer in the act of butchering a pig. At another time he closely pursued a party that was forced to abandoned its sheep and escape. The Bucktails' historian groused, "General Meade, indeed, seems to have had a faculty of appearing where he was not wanted." Patience collapsed when hungry soldiers disrupted the camp, shouting at Meade: "Crackers and Hardtack!" The general ordered the entire division under arms and made them stand in a freezing rain for two hours to cool them off. Eventually, food and clothing arrived, the troops received their back pay, "and the men appeared in most excellent spirits." George Meade's spirits also rose when he received news of his promotion to major general.[7]

The Reserves left Brooks Station on December 8 and moved closer to Fredericksburg. After an all-day ordeal over slippery roads and snow, the men had advanced all of eight miles to White Oak Church. All of the activity around them hinted that Burnside had cooked up a plan. On December 10, officers announced orders for the troops to prepare for battle. They furnished the men with sixty rounds of ammunition and later distributed an additional twenty for safe measure. Everyone assumed their position in the division. One soldier wrote, "every man capable of carrying a musket was ordered to be present in the ranks, even the musicians." Drawing four days' rations, the men cooked three and waited for the inevitable call to advance. Several of the regiments received additional instructions for a very special assignment.[8]

Ambrose Burnside planned to throw pontoon bridges across the Rappahannock on December 11, and strike the Confederates around Fredericksburg before they could concentrate their forces. To protect the engineers constructing these bridges, Burnside detached several regiments to cover the riverfront. Meade picked the 10th Reserves and the sure-shot Bucktails to guard one of the three crossing areas. The two regiments silently quit their camps at 11:30 p.m. and met a passel of pontoons and artillery near Falmouth. Spiriting its way downriver, the group arrived at its destination around 2:00 a.m. While the artillery set up on a bluff known as Stafford Heights, and the engineers prepared to launch their unwieldy pontoons into the icy river, the Reserves dispersed along the river banks. Stationed two miles south of Fredericksburg, the Reserves scanned the darkness for any signs of the Confederates. Convinced that all was safe, the engineers cast off and started lashing their bridges together.[9]

At dawn Confederate skirmishers started peppering the bridge-builders, but the Reserves scattered them easily with a well directed fire. Though driven off, the Southerners continued to hover near the river and the Pennsylvanians maintained a constant vigil against repeated small forays. General Meade reported his men dominated the river without suffering any loss, "although there was considerable firing between our sharpshooters and those of the enemy posted on the opposite bank." The engineers finished their spans by 11:00 a.m.[10]

While the 10th Reserves and the Bucktails shivered along the Rappahannock, George Meade primed the rest of the division for action. The men answered roll call at 3:00 a.m. and started on the road within half an hour. The dark column looked somber as it snaked its way down deeply shadowed roads. "The moon was shining brightly, the air was still and frosty," recalled one Pennsylvanian, "The usual hilarity was lacking and the few words said were spoken in subdued tones." Another one of the Reserves remembered, "the steady tramp of men alone disturbed the death-like stillness of the morning." As the division drew close to the river the men halted in a heavy pine forest, loaded their weapons, and waited for news on the bridges. One soldier took the opportunity to write home, nervously closing: "God only knows where we shall be tonight." Good news of the completed bridges was overshadowed by the constant booming of artillery at the two upper pontoon sites. Burnside refused to let his troops cross below Fredericksburg until he secured the bridges into the city. Afternoon passed into twilight with the Reserves listening to the unabated struggle to finish the bridges upriver. Darkness ended the fighting and the Pennsylvania Reserves retraced its steps for a quarter of a mile to bivouac for the night. Lieutenant Robert Taggert pondered the curious day, noting in his diary, "This had been a noisy day one constant roar of cannon from early morning." Noting the stillness of the night, he concluded, "Strange contrast!"[11]

Burnside's army awoke on December 12 to start the advance anew. The troops crowded toward the river and filed across the pontoons, which bobbed gently under the constant tramp of soldiers. The engineers constructed a third bridge beside the two guarded by the 10th Reserves and the Bucktails. Meade's men shuffled to the crest of Stafford Heights by midmorning and the soldiers overlooked a scene of seeming pandemonium spreading across the river bottoms. Edwin R. Gearhart of the 142nd Pennsylvania wrote, "This large flat was

Division commander **George Gordon Meade,** shown here as a major general. Meade would go on to command the Army of the Potomac from Gettysburg through Appomattox.

Col. William McCandless, commander of the 2nd PA Reserves. Division commander George Meade approached McCandless on the battlefield at Fredericksburg and, pointing to his shoulder straps, asked, "A star this morning, William?" Just then a Confederate shell gutted the colonel's horse. McCandless answered gruffly, "More likely a wooden overcoat." Although he joked of dying on the field, McCandless survived the war.

Evan M. Woodward, adjutant of the 2nd PA Reserves As Burnside's army took position on the plateau prior to its assault at Fredericksburg, Woodward thought "It was one of the most magnificent sights the eyes of man ever rested upon."

All photos courtesy of the Massachusetts M.O.L.L.U.S Collection, USAMHI

Third Brigade commander **Brig. Gen. Conrad F. Jackson,** was a member of the Society of Friends, a religious sect that abhorred all notions of violence. He was living in Virginia when the Civil War broke out, and returned to Pennsylvania to help raise the 9th Reserves—despite the displeasure of his religious community.

Second Brigade commander **Col. William Magilton** had as much military experience as any general at Fredericksburg. He graduated from West Point in the much-touted class of 1846 (along with Stonewall Jackson), and served in the artillery during the War with Mexico and in the Second Seminole War before helping to keep peace in Bleeding Kansas. Despite his credentials, Magilton did not rise through the ranks as rapidly as some of his peers.

First Brigade commander **Col. William Sinclair** gained much of his military experience as an artillerist in the old Regular Army. With the onset of the Civil War, he became an officer and led the 6th PA Reserves. He had assumed command of the First Brigade less than a month before the Battle of Fredericksburg, but Meade showed every confidence in his

All photos courtesy of the Massachusetts
M.O.L.L.U.S Collection, USAMHI

covered with a moving mass of 'blue' flowing out over the bridge, constantly and slowly something like molasses out of a jug."[12] A member of the 121st Pennsylvania described the moment as:

> a magnificent sight, being filled with troops moving some in one direction, some in another, many resting, their arms stacked, awaiting their turns to fall in, officers hurrying to and fro, batteries of artillery and regiments of cavalry mingling with the infantry, all making up an immense mass of humanity that it would seem impossible to prevent being hopelessly mixed and blended together.[13]

The new soldiers marveled at the ease with which the different regiments neatly found order amid chaos and crossed the river with "no confusion whatever being apparent."[14]

The Pennsylvania Reserves swung across the bridges, making a point of marching out of step so as not to upset the pontoons. Arriving on the Confederate side of the Rappahannock, Meade drew his men into line. Once formed, the division climbed out of the bottoms onto a flat, open plain by the "Mannsfield" plantation, the home of Mr. Arthur H. Bernard. As Burnside's army took position on the plateau, Adjutant Woodward of the 2nd Reserves thought "It was one of the most magnificent sights the eyes of man ever rested upon." Maneuvering into the open field probably afforded the Army of the Potomac the first opportunity to see a majority of its forces arrayed for battle. The broken nature of previous battlefields had denied the army a look at itself in action.[15]

Meade's division marched south paralleling the river for a mile. Coming to a deep ravine with a creek, Meade halted and formed line of battle. Holding down the Army of the Potomac's left flank, Meade rested his own left on the Rappahannock and ran his front along the lip of a ravine. His right almost connected with the neighboring division of Brigadier General John Gibbon. Skirmishers dashed across the marshy gorge and approached "Smithfield," the elegant mansion of Dr. Thomas Pratt. The owner had decided to flee from the menacing Federals but left his overseer to defend the property. When the 2nd Reserves discovered the doors barred, they entered through a window. Colonel William McCandless, commander of the 2nd Reserves, arrested the overseer and two other men in the house and sent them to the rear under guard. Some of the 2nd Reserves took advantage of the luxurious dwelling to keep watch in relative warmth that night. Meanwhile, the Bucktails advanced further to the front, sparring with some Confederate cavalry.[16]

At dusk, General Burnside rode down the line and was "received with enthusiasm by the troops." The Pennsylvania Reserves rent the air with hearty cheers as the army commander scanned the Confederate positions. Aware that the Southerners held a series of wooded ridges west and south of Fredericksburg, Burnside decided to launch his main attack against the southern terminus of these hills. As Meade's men bedded down in the winter's cold, they had no idea that Burnside had targeted their front as the point to achieve success on the morrow. "Everything is very quiet this evening," Luther C. Furst noted in his diary, "and no one would suppose for a moment that two large hostile armies were in such close proximity." Furst's only anxiety lay in the hope that "the infernal cannons will keep quiet" so he could "dream of onward to Richmond."[17]

Most of the division's soldiers were too preoccupied to dream of Richmond. Several of the men spent an unsettling night wrestling with premonitions of impending death. A young Quaker named Joseph L. Pratt confided to his friends that this battle would be his last. A Captain in the 1st Reserves offered to let Pratt stay behind but the soldier declined to leave the ranks. Lieutenant Reuben M. Long of the 9th Reserves spent the evening dwelling on his certain death. As friends attempted to change his mind he persisted. The lieutenant calmly maintained, "I feel sure this will be my last night with the boys," and parcelled out his valuables to be sent home. Both Pratt and Long would receive mortal wounds within the next twenty-four hours. Lieutenant Robert Taggert had earlier looked upon the darkened forms of the sleeping soldiers and mused, "I'm afraid that many of the poor fellows now ready to march will never return to camp or home." No one could say what the next day would hold for them. "All wise Providence does not permit us to look into the future," Taggert admitted to his diary, closing with an unconvincing belief, "It is well. All things are well."[18]

On a frozen December 13, George Meade's Pennsylvania Reserves were "up before day break." As the bivouac came to life a number of small encounters snapped the men to attention. An imprudent rabbit unfortunately crossed paths with the 121st Pennsylvania. A mob converged on the spry little creature, which precipitated a good deal of "scrambling and tumbling and hooting among the soldiers." For an instant, the men forgot "all serious thoughts of the coming conflict." A fox that had ventured between the lines drew the unwanted interest of both armies as skirmishers in blue and gray each took a shot at it before it fled. Soon the fire turned more serious. Dismounted Confederate cavalry attacked the Bucktails near the Smithfield house. The fighting grew heavy enough for the Bucktails to need help. Colonel McCandless detached two companies of the 2nd Reserves to bolster the skirmishers but, the action continued to escalate, causing McCandless to move up the balance of his regiment before the situation stabilized. As the Confederates disappeared back into the morning darkness, Meade joined General Reynolds at the Left Grand Division's headquarters.[19]

The generals gathering around William B. Franklin's headquarters at "Mannsfield" puzzled over the lack of orders from Burnside. Shortly after 7:30 a.m. the missing orders arrived. Franklin read Burnside's astonishingly vague and rambling directive which instructed him to "keep your whole command in position for a rapid movement down the old Richmond Road and. . .send. . .a division at least. . .to seize, if possible, the height near Captain Hamilton's. . . taking care to keep it well-supported and its line of retreat open." Burnside's orders lacked the aggressiveness and the clarity that Franklin had expected. He concluded that Burnside intended to land his main attack elsewhere and the left wing should launch a secondary assault to divert the Confederates' attention. Unaware that Burnside still intended Franklin's units to lead the primary effort, the Left Grand Division commander determined to follow Burnside's order to the letter of the law. Franklin ordered Reynolds to prepare one division, well supported, to advance. Reynolds gave the assignment to his most reliable veterans, telling Meade to ready his men. Meade quickly galloped back to his bivouac and the long roll summoned the men into line.[20]

George Meade and John Reynolds rode forward to look at the Confederate-held hills and plot out the attack. The landscape did not look promising. The Pennsylvania Reserves needed to cross a sweeping plain of close to a mile in width. Cutting across the open fields ran peculiar Virginia ditch fences or drainage ditches that were often topped with thick cedars, making it difficult to maintain an alignment. Skirting the far edge of the field ran the Richmond, Fredericksburg, and Potomac Railroad. Beyond the railroad heavy timber covered imposing hills and concealed the Confederates from the Federals' eyes.

The Confederates had busily fortified portions of the hills in front of Meade. Lieutenant General Thomas J. "Stonewall" Jackson's Corps defended this sector, a narrow two-mile front with some 35,000 troops. Jackson had stacked his divisions in three successive lines. This powerful position was marred by one obvious (at least with hindsight) fault: Maj. Gen. A. P. Hill, one of Jackson's division commanders, had left undefended a 600-yard interval of the Confederate front line. This neglected sector consisted of a marshy stand of woods that jutted across the railroad tracks.

The two Northern generals fixed on that thin finger of woods that protruded into the field as the point to guide the attack. Union artillery would pummel the hills to soften up the position before Meade's Pennsylvanians swept forward. Meade had his doubts. He believed he could take the heights but confessed he could not hold them without support. Meade tried to get reinforcements up front but Franklin denied him, merely stating, "That is General Burnside's order."[21]

Meade put his troops in motion "immediately on receiving orders." The head of his column crossed the Smithfield ravine, passed a burnt mill, and marched 800 yards downriver to the "Smithfield" manor. Wheeling right, the men drew into battle line facing west toward the Confederates. Standing in a corn stubble field, the men unslung their knapsacks and threw them in piles. A lucky few fell out of ranks to guard the division's belongings. George Meade placed Col. William Sinclair's First Brigade in front with Col. Albert L. Magilton's Second Brigade 300 yards behind it. Brigadier General Conrad Feger Jackson's Third Brigade remained in column to their left flank.[22]

William Sinclair had gained much of his military experience as an artillerist in the old Regular Army. With the war, he became an officer and led the 6th Reserves. He had assumed command of the First Brigade less than a month before but Meade showed every confidence in his ability. Sinclair deployed his troops with the 1st Reserves on the right, the 2nd on the left, and the untested 121st Pennsylvania in the center. Sinclair detailed his own 6th Reserves as skirmishers and gave the much used Bucktails of the 13th Reserves a rest. The Bucktails prepared to stand in support of the artillery.[23]

Colonel Albert L. Magilton had as much military experience as any general at Fredericksburg. He had graduated from West Point in the highly vaunted class of 1846 along with Stonewall Jackson. He had served in the artillery during the War with Mexico and in the Second Seminole War. He had helped keep peace in Bleeding Kansas and undertook the rigors of teaching in the Philadelphia public school system. Despite his credentials, Magilton had failed to rise with his peers and had led a brigade slightly longer than Sinclair. Magilton's line formed with the novice 142nd Pennsylvania holding the right, followed by the 8th, 4th, 3rd, and 7th Reserves.[24]

Brigadier General Conrad Feger Jackson sacrificed much to lead his troops onto the battlefield. As a member of the Society of Friends, a religious sect that abhorred all notions of violence, Jackson had directed his early life to peaceful pursuits, working in warehouses, railroads, and the revenue service. His first taste of the martial world came with delivering dispatches to the U.S. Army during the War with Mexico. Living in Virginia when the Civil War broke out,

Jackson returned to Pennsylvania and helped raise the 9th Reserves despite the displeasure of his religious community. Wounded at Second Manassas, Jackson had earned a general's star and the command of the Third Brigade. His men remained in column in the likely order of the 11th Reserves in front, trailed by the 5th, 12th, and 10th Reserves. The 9th Reserves spread out as skirmishers to their left.[25]

Satisfied that everyone was in position, Meade ordered Sinclair forward to the old Richmond Road (also known as the Richmond Stage Road or Bowling Green Road) to clear off a heavy growth of cedars and bridge the ditches lining the road. The men advanced to the road and commenced tearing down the hedges. Meade reported that "some time was consumed in removing the hedge fences on this road, and bridging the drains on each side for the passage of artillery." Some of the Reserves thought that "considerable time was lost" making the path passable for the division and its guns.[26]

While his brigade struggled with the brush, Sinclair pushed his 6th Reserves beyond the road to drive off the Confederate skirmishers. Soon after, Meade looked up to see Sinclair's brigade had advanced across the road and 300 yards into the open fields. Meade became excited because Sinclair had ventured so far ahead without artillery support. Riding rapidly to the road, Meade cried, "Good God! How came that brigade out here? No artillery—no supports!" Staff officers hustled to rush the rest of the division and its cannon forward. Just as the last of the Reserves passed into the field a lone cannon boomed out close to the left.[27]

The first shot of the Battle of Fredericksburg echoed through the air at 10:00 a.m. A lazy shot arched across the sky from left to right and buried itself in the muddy field before the Reserves. Bates Alexander of the 7th Reserves recalled:

> When thus standing in line a cannon boomed out on our left, at close range, seemingly on the Bowling Green road, a shot whizzed high in the air passing over our heads from left to right along the line. Naturally supposing, from the position, 'twas one of our own batteries. We thought our gunners had had too much 'commissary' this morning and so remarked.[28]

When the harmless round was followed by a steady stream of shots, the Reserves cut short their jokes of drunken cannoneers. Confederate Major John Pelham had placed a gun squarely on the Federal left flank and fired down the ranks of Meade's division. Officers yelled for the men to lay down in the mud for safety. General Reynolds ordered C. Feger Jackson's brigade to face left into line, staring directly at Pelham's position. Federal artillery raced to the front and dropped trails to deal with the Confederate menace.[29]

The Pennsylvanians laid in cold, clinging mud for close to an hour enduring the fire. The soldiers maintained "perfect silence" even though they "suffered terribly" in their exposed position. The destructive fire hurt a number of men. The 121st Pennsylvania suffered seven casualties to one shot. Another round cut a man in two. Company D of the 11th Reserves lost its last officer mortally wounded by one of Pelham's bolts. As Captain William Stewart's men carried him off the field, the officer begged them "to go into the impending struggle as bravely as if he were with them." At one point, a body of Confederate sharpshooters crept along the hedges of the old Richmond Road and "kept up a galling fire" on C. Feger Jackson's brigade. Jackson detached two companies to drive the Southerners away. By 11:00 a.m. the sharpshooters had melted back into the landscape and Pelham packed up his artillery. Meade readied his troops to begin the attack. Northern batteries reformed to face Prospect Hill while C. Feger Jackson's brigade wheeled right to come into line as an extension of Sinclair's First Brigade battle line.[30]

The Northern artillery turned its full might against the Confederate stronghold on the ridge. Cannon ranged back and forth, pounding "Stonewall" Jackson's Southerners. Meade's men continued to lie in the mud, listening to the ferocious bark of the guns. Some of the stiff infantrymen complained about their uncomfortable, waterlogged uniforms. "The men were dingy and muddy as turtles," Edwin Gearhart grumbled, consoling himself that even "the officers' uniforms had lost their shining qualities." Others made the best of the situation and caught up on some much needed sleep. Some of the troops worried about what the Confederates had waiting in store for them. An observant few noted that the Southerners "preserved an ominous silence" throughout the barrage. After an hour, the artillerists suspected it was time for the Pennsylvania Reserves to charge the hill.[31]

Officers ordered the men onto their feet. Lunging forward, the whole line hurried over the exposed flatland. As the line swept to within 800 yards of Prospect Hill, Confederate artillery opened a surprise plunging fire that wreaked havoc with the Pennsylvanians. Shells tore through the packed ranks and the attack began to falter. The Southerners fired so accurately that one of Meade's men assumed that stakes found in the field had been planted by the enemy as range markers. As momentum failed and the line began to collapse, Meade ordered the troops to lie down again. The Federal artillery lashed its guns to the front once more and reopened its bombardment.[32]

The artillery of both armies grappled in a deadly duel to gain control of the open fields south of Fredericksburg. The Pennsylvania Reserves huddled in the mud and the slop while angry shells shrieked and whistled across the landscape. "Now the dogs of war are being let loose," Luther Furst of the 10th Reserves fretted, "and the rebs are throwing their rotten shells all around us, much to our discomfort." The 2nd Reserves adjutant wrote that many of the deadly missiles "plowed up the earth in deep furrows, or went howling and bursting over our heads, filling the air with iron hail and sulphur." Some of the shots landing among the Reserves kicked up spigots of mud "higher than the tallest tree," while others bounded through the ranks like grotesque rubber balls. "This is the most trying position soldiers can be placed in," one veteran observed. A novice in the 121st Pennsylvania confessed, "There is certainly something very terrifying in such accompaniments that had not a great tendency to strengthen the nerves." The mental torture as well as the physical punishment unnerved a number of men. "To remain quiet under such a fire," a seasoned infantryman testified, "was more trying than active conflict with the foe." Several of the experienced men appeared even more frightened than they wished to let on. Captain Hugh McDonald of the Bucktail regiment feared the Confederates hurled everything under the sun at him, desponding, "The rebels fired grape, canister, shells, railroad iron, and parts of plow shares."[33]

John Reynolds and George Meade moved among the troops to raise the troops' morale. General Reynolds stayed close to the uninitiated men of the 142nd Pennsylvania to calm them through the trying ordeal. The First Corps commander must have wondered at the rookies who not only behaved well under fire but actually jumped up and cheered when their sickly Col. Robert Cummins hobbled onto the battlefield to resume command of his regiment. General Meade rode slowly from regiment to regiment, chatting pleasantly with the officers and men. Approaching Col. William McCandless of the 2nd Reserves, Meade pointed to his shoulder straps and volunteered, "A star this morning, William?" Just then a Confederate shell gutted the colonel's horse. McCandless answered gruffly, "More likely a wooden overcoat." Wherever Meade encountered the dead lying amid the living, he demanded that the body be immediately buried so the men did not linger on the loss.[34]

As Meade talked with his men he kept an eye on the Confederate bastion, looking for an opportunity to renew his attack. At 1:00 p.m. he knew the time had arrived. A couple of Federal artillery rounds hit two Southern ammunition chests and touched off a furious explosion. The Reserves leapt to their feet and cheered the impressive show of pyrotechnics. Meade seized the moment and shouted at the men to charge. Amid loud cheers, officers ordered the men to fix bayonets. Colonel William Sinclair led the First Brigade past the batteries and his men sprang forward into a run, beginning what one participant called, "the most gallant charge of the war."[35]

The Reserves surged across the field amid a torrent of Confederate shells. George W. McCracken of the 10th Reserves reported that the division pressed ahead "as though its ranks were not being plowed by shot and shell." Bates Alexander thought that the firestorm was worse than in the Miller cornfield at Antietam, and remarked, "Hell itself had broke loose again." The men inclined their heads as if breasting a driving rain and instinctively crowded toward the center of the line. Edward Steffen kept a constant pace, explaining, "Even if the man directly in front of you falls upon the ground, you do not notice him, you run right over him." The ranks became so compact that a flushed rabbit darted up and down the line before it could nudge its way to the rear. The wave of soldiers rolled across the open span when it suddenly plunged into a ditch "about five feet deep with nearly perpendicular sides, and water and ice at the bottom." Many of the soldiers tumbled in unexpectedly and crawled out the other side. Others jumped the ditch, then a second, and a third, as the sea of bluecoats closed in on the railroad.[36]

George Meade watched Sinclair's and Jackson's men race for the railroad. When he turned to check on Magilton's progress, he spied the unemployed Bucktails supporting the artillery. Riding up to their commander, Capt. Charles F. Taylor, Meade demanded that the regiment catch up with Sinclair's brigade. Taylor pointed his men toward the division's right when he saw a gap opening up near the left center. Several of the units in Jackson's brigade had started diverging but the Bucktails shifted left and neatly sealed the gap.[37]

William Sinclair's soldiers struck the center of the belt of woods that jutted out from the railroad. As the men disappeared into the foliage they found themselves bogged down in a marshy wetland studded with thick oaks and dwarf pines. Hacking their way forward, momentum carried them to the railroad. Albert Magilton's men followed Sinclair's path and closed to within 100 yards of the First Brigade's rear. Meanwhile, C. Feger Jackson dashed ahead of the other two brigades, traversing cleared ground to the left of the marsh. Arriving at the railroad ahead of Sinclair's men, Jackson's troops met a devastating fire from Confederate infantry posted on the hilltop beyond the tracks. Jackson's men scampered into the ditches along the railroad and returned the

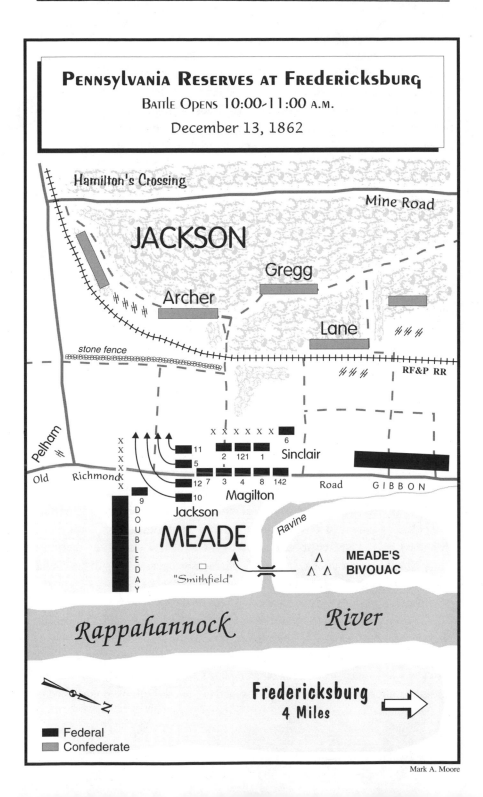

Mark A. Moore

fire, shooting over the embankment. The Confederate musketry threw the Federals into confusion. C. Feger Jackson's right inclined toward the cover of the marsh while the center held the railroad grade and the left regiment, the 9th Reserves, lay trapped behind a small stone fence 100 yards shy of the railroad. The general may not have known that the Bucktails plugged the gap between his right regiment, the 11th Reserves, and the center of his brigade. Jackson attempted to reorder his line, riding back and forth, exhorting the troops, "Rally men, rally right here."[38]

While Jackson tried to straighten out his line, Sinclair's men eased across the railroad without encountering any resistance. The Confederates had left a 600-yard space in their front unprotected, surmising that it was impassible for an organized force. Sinclair's brigade happened into the heart of that gap by luck. Swarming up the wooded hillside, the men could see only a few yards ahead so they proceeded cautiously.[39]

Magilton's brigade crowded toward Sinclair's rear, with regiments overlapping both of the First Brigade's flanks. Magilton could not see Sinclair ahead of him but assumed that the forward units covered his entire front. When the 142nd Pennsylvania, his new regiment on the right, encountered the Confederates north of the marsh, Colonel Magilton ordered it not to return fire. Certain that the 142nd would hurt their friends in front, Magilton left his right powerless under "a terrific and galling fire." Troops on their left had the benefit of the trees for cover but the 142nd lay "entirely at the mercy of the enemy. . .who took the best advantage of it." The regiment suffered the highest casualties of the division and lost both its major and adjutant to wounds. Major Silas M. Baily's 8th Reserves tried to help the rookies by turning the Confederate defenses along the railroad. Caught in a severe firefight Baily fell wounded and his adjutant was killed. The veterans reported, "Never before had it been subjected to so terrible an ordeal." Regardless of the intense fighting on the division's north flank, Magilton never bothered to ascertain why his right had stalled. At the same time, Magilton's left thronged into C. Feger Jackson's rear, adding to the confusion. Only Sinclair's men appeared to be making any headway.[40]

Sinclair's troops clawed their way through the dense thicket and brush. The uneven ground and undergrowth rapidly destroyed the brigade's alignment. Meade declared that the "regiments separated from brigades, and companies from regiments" as they struggled over the natural obstructions. Adding to the muddle was the lack of a strong directing hand. Colonel Sinclair never made it past the railroad. Receiving a painful wound in the left heel, the colonel had to be borne to the rear. Colonel William McCandless inherited the command, but he had advanced deep into the woods and was unaware of the change.[41]

Rising to the crest of the ridge, the Federals blundered into a Confederate brigade resting in reserve. Henry Flick wrote that the bluecoats closed in quietly which added to the surprise. The 1st and 6th Reserves fell upon the unsuspecting Southerner brigade "with wild yells" and began "scattering it like chaff" before the Confederates could reclaim their stacked weapons. The action was quick and decisive. General Maxcy Gregg's South Carolina brigade retreated pell-mell through the underbrush with the Reserves in hot pursuit. Following the broken Confederates, the 1st and 6th Reserves wheeled right and expanded the breakthrough northward.

These two regiments linked up with Magilton's 4th and 8th Reserves who had penetrated the woods but could not bypass the obstinate Confederate defenders north of the marsh. Together, these regiments still failed to drive away the Southerners who pinned the 142nd Pennsylvania on the railroad. At the same time, the rest of the First Brigade pressed deeper into the Confederate rear. The 2nd Reserves and 121st Pennsylvania lost contact with the rest of the brigade and pretty soon lost contact with each other.[42]

The wedge of troops pouring through the marsh relieved some of the pressure on C. Feger Jackson's troops. From a position behind Magilton's line, George Meade saw that Jackson needed to get his men under the cover of the woods. The division commander dispatched orders to Jackson and may have sent Colonel Magilton to mind his own brigade's left.[43]

General Jackson came to the same conclusion Meade had. Riding toward the center of his line Jackson encouraged the 5th Reserves to sidle to the left. Confederates fixed on the large general dashing behind the line on a beautiful white horse. A hail of bullets killed the horse and plunged the officer to the ground. Jackson drew his sword and jumped onto the railroad. Just then, Meade's aide, Lieutenant Arthur Dehon drew rein before the general. The staff officer immediately fell dead with a bullet through his chest. Jackson turned to point his men to the woods when another volley swept half his staff out of the saddle. At that moment, Conrad Feger Jackson fell dead with a bullet hole drilled through his head. The soldiers of the 5th Reserves surged instinctively for the cover of the trees while the 12th and 10th Reserves maintained their positions along the embankment. The far left 9th Reserves sat tight, unable to rejoin the brigade. Their leader, Lt. Colonel Robert Anderson should have assumed command of the brigade but he had no way of getting to the railroad and probably did not know of Jackson's death until later.[44]

Magilton's left overlapped Jackson's brigade and scurried toward the marsh with the jumbled mass in front of them. Heading for the left, Magilton's horse collapsed from a crippling wound and the brigade commander completely lost touch with his men. The 7th Reserves took its cue from a reckless soldier named James McCauley, who hopped onto the embankment and halloed, "Wide awake fellows, let's give 'em hell!" The regiment "rushed wildly for the wood" amid the frightening hum of canister. The 7th lost two color bearers before entering the trees. Bates Alexander confessed, "I could run at such times like a scared deer." The horde of soldiers fumbling through the woods and swamp moved in every direction "in a sort of helter-skelter way." Not one of Meade's brigade commanders had penetrated beyond the railroad to organize the advance. The men pushed ahead by impulse rather than direction.[45]

Parts of the Federal units splintering in the woods followed Adjutant Evan M. Woodward as he headed south along the ridge top. Woodward broke off from the rest of the 2nd Reserves and pushed toward the Southerners harassing Jackson's Third Brigade. Woodward picked up elements of the 11th Reserves and smashed into the Confederate brigade of James J. Archer. Locking onto the Southerners' exposed left flank, Woodward's men fired down the length of the Confederate earthworks. Woodward's group closed across the rear of their enemy while portions of the 7th Reserves, 5th Reserves, and the Bucktails hammered the works from the slope of the hill in front. Evan Woodward realized that the Federals had crossed their fire and he started taking casualties from friendly bluecoats. Running ahead, Woodward dove into the Confederate trench. Surrounded by over a hundred Southerners, Woodward asked them if they cared to surrender. They answered, "We will surrender, if you will let us." Quieting the fire, Woodward removed his prisoners down the hill and secured the battle-flag of the 19th Georgia—the only Confederate flag captured at Fredericksburg. Woodward refused to leave the front with his trophies so he detached Charles Upjohn to carry the flag to the rear. When Upjohn fell wounded, Jacob Cart of the 7th Reserves took the flag. The Congress rewarded Cart with the Medal of Honor. Thirty years later, a Medal of Honor was bestowed on Woodward as well.[46]

The Pennsylvania Reserves fragmented inside the gap, pressing in every direction and expanding the breach. Meade wrote "the attack was for a time perfectly successful." As the Federals pierced the Confederate defenses, they exploded the hole to twice its size. The impetus, however, was rapidly diminishing. Casualties escalated and much of the leadership had fallen. On the right, the 4th Reserves lost its commander when Lt. Col. Richard H. Woolworth was

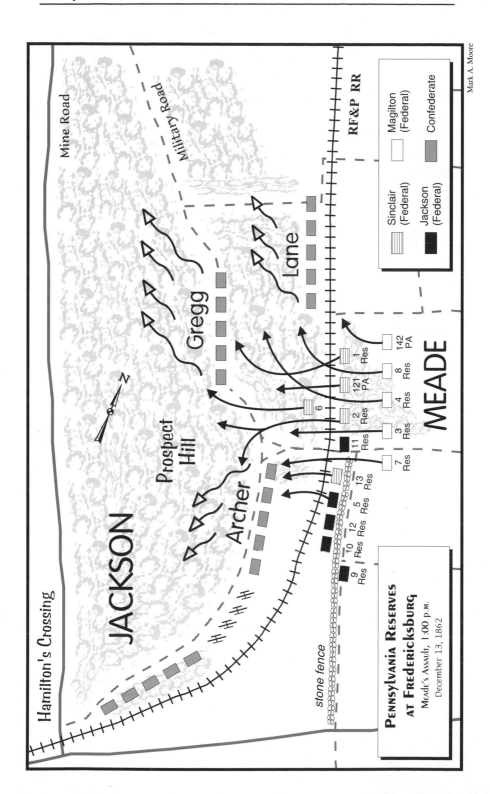

Mark A. Moore

Mine Road

Military Road

RF&P RR

Sinclair (Federal)

Magilton (Federal)

Jackson (Federal)

Confederate

JACKSON

Hamilton's Crossing

Prospect Hill

Gregg

Lane

Archer

N

stone fence

142 PA

8 Res

1 Res

121 PA

4 Res

6

2 Res

3 Res

7 Res

11 Res

13 Res

5 Res

12 Res

10 Res

9 Res

MEADE

PENNSYLVANIA RESERVES AT FREDERICKSBURG
MEADE'S ASSAULT, 1:00 P.M.
December 13, 1862

carried off wounded. On the left, Col. Henry C. Bolinger of the 7th Reserves hopped off Prospect Hill, nursing a wounded ankle. The Bucktails' leader, Capt. Charles F. Taylor had one horse shot out from under him and soon fell with a bullet through his shoulder. His replacement, Capt. Edward A. Irvin also fell wounded. The 5th Reserves lost its entire leadership with Lt. Col. George Dare dropping wounded, Maj. Frank Zentmeyer mortally wounded and captured, and his brother, acting adjutant David Zentmeyer dying in the vortex of the battle. Only Evan Woodward and George Meade seemed to lead charmed lives. Woodward survived the day without a scratch, though Confederate bullets had perforated his uniform thirteen times. General Meade found himself surrounded by deadly missiles. A Southern ball ripped through the crown of the general's wide-brimmed hat while another passed through the neck of his horse. A new threat to Meade wore a blue uniform. The general spied a skulker bolting for the rear. As he rode down the soldier Meade saw the man level his rifle at him. Impulsively, the general throttled the bluecoat with the flat of his sword, breaking the blade down to the hilt. Meade sent the bewildered man back to the front with angry curses ringing in his ears.[47]

The Pennsylvania Reserves' attack had reached its zenith. Meade dispatched a staff officer to bring forward reinforcements to secure his gains. The aide sought help from the closest troops at hand. Appealing to Brigadier General David B. Birney, Meade's officer was astounded when Birney declined to help. Birney commanded a Third Corps division sent to cooperate with the First Corps. Birney accepted orders from the corps commander, John Reynolds, but he did not recognize requests from Reynolds' subordinates. When Meade heard this, he sent another staffer to demand Birney come forward at once. Birney refused again. George Meade's temper erupted. "Meade was almost wild with rage as he saw the golden opportunity slipping away," remembered one soldier. The general raced back to find Birney. Cornering the ignoble division officer, Meade savaged him with blistering curses that could "almost make the stones creep." The major general tartly pointed out that the brigadier needed to follow superior's orders and then snarled, "General, I assume the authority of ordering you up to the relief of my men." Birney gladly complied. Unfortunately, Birney's assistance was too little help and too late, because the Confederates also had sought supports and they had not run into obstinate roadblocks like Birney.[48]

Meade returned to the railroad only to see his success start to crumble. Confederate counterattacks pitched into his left and right flanks and his tenuous hold on the hill began to collapse. As the veteran Reserves bolted down the hillside and over the railroad, they shouted at the 142nd Pennsylvania to "Get out of this, the 'Johnnies' are right behind us!" The entire horde dispersed from the tracks. One soldier recalled, "I remembered when I began to run back," but then caught himself, "retreat (I should say) I was making. . .a speed of at least ten miles per hour." Meanwhile the left started backpeddling under intense pressure. Lieutenant Daniel R. Coder of the 11th Reserves conceded, "Never did I look back for support with more anxiety than on that fatal day." With their ammunition exhausted and no help in sight, the Reserves broke under vicious assaults. "The next instant the gallant boys were almost flying. . .through the bushes," recalled Bates Alexander, who averred, "this was one of my good days for running." Many of the Southerners chased after the bluecoats while others closed in on the center.[49]

Wandering alone in the center, the 121st Pennsylvania lost touch with everyone. Suddenly, the Confederates struck the regiment from the front and the rear and the Northerners quit the hill and fell back to the railroad looking for help. The 3rd Reserves climbed the heights a short distance away and saw the 121st Pennsylvania retreat without the new men detecting the veterans. The 3rd Reserves continued forward and linked up with the 2nd Reserves when both units were assailed from opposite directions. The fighting degenerated into a "desperate hand-to-hand struggle." Colonel Horatio Sickels of the 3rd Reserves had a dozen holes in his coat and his binoculars smashed before it was over. The Federals appeared to be "at the mercy of their assailants" when Southern troops started encircling them. To the beleaguered Reserves it appeared "the foe was swarming on all sides." The 2nd and 3rd Reserves withdrew and slipped out of the closing trap.[50]

Meade attempted to collect his forces along the railroad bed. He seized the colors of the 121st Pennsylvania and the 2nd Reserves as the points for the men to rally. Before the division could reorganize, the Confederates sailed down the ridge and washed over the embankment. Another rare moment of close combat flared before the Reserves fell back across the field. The 9th Reserves covered the retreat from their stone wall stronghold.[51]

The Pennsylvania Reserves rolled back like a resistless tide. General Reynolds joined General Meade and both officers attempted to stem the retreat. Meade stormed back and forth trying to halt various knots of men only to watch them vanish moments later. The survivors of the 121st Pennsylvania noted that the general "seemed considerably vexed." The 4th Reserves found out the hard way. When Captain Enos L. Christman failed to stop his men, "Meade cursed him and told him he would have him shot" if he did not do better. A witness wrote darkly that "Meade is a rough customer when under fire." The remnants of the division pushed through the fastidious ranks of Birney's division. "The men appeared sullen and disheartened," according to a Third Corps officer, "as if they had been badly treated and sacrificed." When an unsullied staff officer ordered the Reserves to rally around him, one dirty veteran flung his rifle in the air and sneered, "I've had enough of this sort of damned business." When another soldier was asked where his unit was, he replied sadly, "Busted up and gone to hell."[52]

The broken pieces of the division gathered near the Smithfield ravine shortly after 2:30 p.m. Ragged soldiers rooted through piles looking for their knapsacks; wounded men writhed in pain outside makeshift hospitals and officers congregated to make sense of the attack. George Meade was incensed at the lack of support. "My God General Reynolds," he exploded, "did they think my division could whip Lee's entire army?" Meade calmed down somewhat by the time William Franklin talked to him. When the Left Grand Division commander acted surprised that the fighting was so desperate, Meade passively fingered the fresh holes in his hat and muttered, "I found it quite hot for me." The division entered the battle with nearly 4,500 troops. Several hours later it reported 1,823 casualties and the loss of two brigade commanders. The remaining 2,600 men saw no further action at Fredericksburg. The division regrouped during the night and stood in line on December 14. The battle lines North and South glared at each other through "a long, weary day of expectancy." December 15 saw more of the same.[53]

Soon after dark on December 15, as the first drops of rain washed the blood stained battlefield, officers ordered the men under arms. Details built camp fires while the men silently crept toward the pontoon crossings. "Not a word was spoke. The canteens, cups, and accouterments did not rattle and jingle as usually," remembered Luther C. Furst, "and all seemed to be conscious that on the silence depended their lives." The Reserves crossed on bridges covered in sod and brush to muffle the noise. The dejected shadow of the old Pennsylvania Reserves slipped over the Rappahannock River to safety and shuffled into its old camp around White Oak Church.[54]

The division was little stronger than a small brigade and morale plummeted in the aftermath of Fredericksburg. Lieutenant Robert Taggert of the 9th Reserves voiced the opinion of many when he declared, "The expedition [was] a failure. . . .The undertaking seemed like madness." The Reserves took the loss harder than most. Evan Woodward lamented, "The battle of Fredericksburg was lost, the bright hopes of the Nation and the army are blasted, and the victory that was within our grasp was gone forever." John B. Tobias of the 8th Reserves agreed that this was a despicable trend, writing, "our victory was snatched away and defeat fell to our lot again." The soldiers of the Pennsylvania Reserves believed they had come close to accomplishing the impossible. One veteran summed up the action, stating, "General Meade had come within a hair's breadth of achieving a great success."[55]

Contrary to all the historical attention lavished on the December 13 action around Marye's Heights and the stone wall, these Confederate defenses did not determine the outcome of the Battle of Fredericksburg. The Federals suffered predictable losses against them without one soldier even reaching the Southern lines, much less penetrating them. The decisive factor of the battle focused on the fighting around Prospect Hill. George Gordon Meade's Pennsylvania Reserves fought the true Battle of Fredericksburg, as opposed to the dramatic and compelling slaughter of Federal troops that took place on the Federal right. A soldier in the 121st Pennsylvania summarized the difference:

> The dreadful slaughter in front of Marye's Hill at no time approached success, but, however brave, the efforts of the troops at that point were from the first utterly hopeless. Meade's were the only troops that broke through the enemy's lines, and saw victory, for a short time, perched upon their banners.[56]

General George Meade sadly noted that the difference for him "made me feel worse. . .than if we had been repulsed from the first."[57]

Endnotes

1. Edward W. Steffen, February 2, 1863 letter, Fredericksburg and Spotsylvania National Military Park (hereafter cited as FRSP).

2. Charles Henry Veil, reminiscence, Civil War Miscellaneous Collection (hereafter cited as C.W. Misc. Coll.), United States Army Military History Institute (hereafter cited USAMHI); Evan M. Woodward, *Our Campaigns* (Philadelphia, 1865), p. 224.

3. Edward W. Steffen, Nov. 24, 1862 letter, FRSP.

4. Theodore Lyman, *Meade's Headquarters 1863-1865* (Boston, 1922) p. 73; Richard Meade Bache, *Life of George Gordon Meade* (Philadelphia, 1897) p. 571. Meade was

normally a quiet gentleman who once observed that any woman would rather have her husband sworn at than prayed over.

5. Survivors' Association, *History of the 121st Regiment Pennsylvania Volunteers* (Philadelphia, 1893) p. 23; Woodward, *Our Campaigns*, pp. 226-227; Samuel P. Bates, *History of Pennsylvania Volunteers*, 5 vols. (Harrisburg, 1869-1871) vol. 1, p. 669.

6. Bates, *History of Pennsylvania Volunteers*, 1, p. 551; *121st Pennsylvania*, p. 23.

7. Horatio N. Warren, *Two Reunions of the 142nd Regiment of Pa. Vols.* (Buffalo, 1890) pp. 17-18; Diary of Franklin Boyts, Boyts Papers, Historical Society of Pennsylvania; Howard Thomson and William H. Rauch, *History of the Bucktails*, (Phila., 1906) pp. 225-226; Woodward, *Our Campaigns*, p. 227.

8. Diary of Luther C. Furst, Harrisburg Civil War Round Table Collection (hereafter cited as HCWRT Coll.), USAMHI; Diary of Robert Taggert, C. W. Misc. Coll., USAMHI; *121st Pennsylvania Survivors*, p. 24; Diary of Samuel M. Jackson, HCWRT Coll., USAMHI.

9. Taggert diary, USAMHI; Bates, *History of Pennsylvania Volunteers*, 1, p. 851; [Clearfield, Pa.] *Raftman's Journal*, January 7, 1863; Jackson diary, USAMHI; *Beaver Weekly Argus*, December 24, 1862. Some of the 10th Reserves may have helped the pontooniers lay the bridges.

10. Taggert diary, USAMHI; *Raftman's Journal*, January 7, 1863; *The War of the Rebellion: A Compilation of the Official Records of the Union and Confederate Armies*, 128 vols. (Washington, 1880-1901) Series 1, vol. 21, pp. 510, 521. Hereinafter cited as *OR*. All references are to Series 1, vol. 21.

11. *121st Pennsylvania*, p. 24; Woodward, *Our Campaigns*, p. 230; Edwin R. Gearhart, "Reminiscences of the Civil War," *The Spur*, vol. 6, no. 12 (March 1956), p. 16; R. K. Halsey, December 11, 1862 letter, Clements Library, University of Michigan; Taggert diary, USAMHI.

12. *Raftman's Journal*, January 7, 1863; Gearhart, *Spur*, 6, no. 12, p. 16.

13. *121st Pennsylvania*, pp. 24-25.

14. Ibid., p. 25.

15. Woodward, *Our Campaigns*, p. 232; *121st Pennsylvania*, p. 26.

16. Woodward, *Our Campaigns*, p. 232; *OR* 21, p. 510; Philadelphia Inquirer, December 25, 1862; Thomson and Rauch, *History of the Bucktails*, p. 229. Woodward is the only source unearthed that mentions that the Smithfield ravine was bridged.

17. Thomson and Rauch, *History of the Bucktails*, p. 230; Diary of Jacob Heffelfinger, diary, *Civil War Times Illustrated* Collection, USAMHI; *121st Pennsylvania*, p. 26; Furst diary, USAMHI. Thomson and Rauch place Burnside's arrival at 5:00 p.m.

18. Douglas R. Harper, *"If Thee Must Fight": A Civil War History of Chester County, Pennsylvania* (West Chester, 1990) pp. 181-182; Robert Taggert, in *Pennsylvania at Gettysburg*, 4 vols. (Harrisburg, 1893) vol. 1, p. 231; Taggert diary, USAMHI.

19. Taggert diary, USAMHI; *121st Pennsylvania Survivors*, p. 26; Clarence Poe, ed., *True Tales of the South at War* (Chapel Hill, n.d.) p. 89; Woodward, *Our Campaigns*, p. 233; Bates, *History of Pennsylvania Volunteers*, 1, p. 585.

20. *OR* 21, p. 510; Frank A. O'Reilly, *"Stonewall" Jackson at Fredericksburg*, (Lynchburg, 1993), pp. 32-33.

21. James H. Wilson, ed., *The Life and Services of Brevet Brigadier-General Andrew Jonathan Alexander* (New York, 1887), p. 118; Woodward, *Our Campaigns*, p. 238; Charles S. Wainwright, *A Diary of Battle* (New York, 1962), p. 143.

22. *OR* 21, pp. 510, 521; Thomson and Rauch, *History of the Bucktails*, p. 231; *121st Pennsylvania Survivors*, p. 26; Gearhart, Spur, VI, no. 12, p. 17; Samuel Coplan, "Samuel Coplan and the Civil War," reminiscence, possession of Herb Rogers, copy in FRSP; *Philadelphia Inquirer*, December 25, 1862.

23. William Sinclair, Compiled Service Record (hereinafter cited as CSR), National Archives (hereafter cited as NA); J. R. Sypher, *History of the Pennsylvania Reserve Corps* (Lancaster, 1865), p. 407; *OR* 21, p. 518.

24. Sypher, *Pennsylvania Reserve Corps*, pp. 121-123; Bates, *History of Pennsylvania Volunteers*, 4, p. 464; *OR* 21, p. 520.

25. Conrad Feger Jackson, CSR, NA; Sypher, pp. 416-417; O'Reilly, *Jackson at Fredericksburg*, pp. 50, 203. No order of regiments is specifically stated, but see O'Reilly for notes on the probable alignment.

26. *Philadelphia Inquirer*, December 25, 1862; *OR* 21, p. 510; Thomson and Rauch, *History of the Bucktails*, p. 231.

27. Bates, *History of the Pennsylvania Volunteers*, 1, p. 699; George E. Jepson, *Boston Journal*, December 13, 1892; Bates Alexander, *Hummelstown, The Sun*, October 25, 1895.

28. Alexander, *Sun*, October 25, 1895.

29. *121st Pennsylvania*, p. 26; *Raftman's Journal*, January 7, 1863; *OR* 21, p. 511.

30. *OR* 21, p. 522; *Philadelphia Inquirer*, December 25, 1862; *121st Pennsylvania*, p. 27; Bates, *History of Pennsylvania Volunteers*, 1, pp. 852, 884; George W. McCracken, *Pennsylvania at Gettysburg*, vol. I, p. 248.

31. Gearhart, *Spur*, 7, no. 2, (May, 1956), p. 16; *Raftman's Journal*, January 7, 1863.

32. *Raftman's Journal*, January 7, 1862; "Record of Henry Flick," HCWRT Coll., USAMHI, p. 11.

33. Furst diary, USAMHI; Woodward, *Our Campaigns*, p. 235; Alexander, *Sun*, November 3, 1895; Bates, *History of Pennsylvania Volunteers*, 1, p. 727; *121st Pennsyl-*

vania, p. 27; Edwin A. Glover, *Bucktailed Wildcats: A Regiment of Civil War Volunteers* (New York, 1960), p. 176.

34. Bates, *History of Pennsylvania Volunteers*, 4, p. 465; Captain George R. Snowden in Horatio N. Warren, *Two Reunions of the 142nd Regiment Pennsylvania Volunteers* (Buffalo, 1890), p. 51; Gearhart, *Spur*, 6, no. 12, p. 17; St. Clair A. Mulholland, in *Philadelphia Weekly Times*, April 23, 1881; Woodward, *Our Campaigns*, p. 244; Alexander, *Sun*, October 25, 1895.

35. *121st Pennsylvania*, p. 28; Evan M. Woodward, *History of the Third Pennsylvania Reserves* (Trenton, 1883), p. 208; *Philadelphia Inquirer*, December 25, 1862; W. H. H. Gore, *Pennsylvania at Gettysburg*, vol. 1, p. 222.

36. McCracken, *Pennsylvania at Gettysburg*, vol. 1, p. 248; Alexander, *Sun*, November 3, 1895; Gearhart, *Spur*, 7, no. 1, (April, 1956), p. 16; *OR* 21, p. 519.

37. Thomson and Rauch, *History of the Bucktails*, p. 233; *OR* 21, p. 518.

38. Alexander, *Sun*, November 3, 1895; Bates, *History of Pennsylvania Volunteers*, 1, pp. 791, 919; Adam S. Bright, in Aida C. Truxall, *Respects to All: Letters of Two Pennsylvania Boys in the War of the Rebellion* (Pittsburgh, 1962), p. 35; J. O. Kerbey, *On the Warpath* (Chicago,1890), p. 134.

39. *Philadelphia Inquirer*, December 25, 1862; Bates, *History of Pennsylvania Volunteers*, 1, p. 551; Kerbey, *On the Warpath*, p. 133; Evan M. Woodward, CSR, NA.

40. Bates, *History of Pennsylvania Volunteers*, 1, p. 762; ibid., 4, p. 465; Boyts diary, HSPA; Alexander, *Sun*, November 3, 1895.

41. *OR*, p. 513; Bates, *History of Pennsylvania Volunteers*, 1, p. 699; Sinclair CSR, NA.

42. Flick, USAMHI; *OR* 21, p. 519; Woodward, *3rd Pennsylvania Reserves*, p. 208.

43. Thomson and Rauch, *History of the Bucktails*, p. 234; *OR* 21, p. 512.

44. Kerbey, *On the Warpath*, p. 134; Sypher, *Pennsylvania Reserve Corps*, p. 417; *Philadelphia Inquirer*, December 25, 1862; Charles S. Wainwright, *War Journal*, vol. 1, Huntington Library. The *Inquirer* reported that Jackson's "fatal shot entered the right temple, near the eye of the General, and passed through his head and out behind the left ear." An alternate version, reported by Wainwright, noted that Jackson, "was sitting down at the time, either so confused, or worse, that he could go no farther."

45. Alexander, *Sun*, November 3, 1895; *OR* 21, p. 521. Alexander of the 7th Reserves encountered Magilton on the left: "Below the fence Col. Magilton's horse had been struck and he was holding it by the bridle while it vainly endeavored to raise." Magilton was further hampered by the loss of two of his staff officers wounded.

46. Woodward CSR, NA; Woodward, *Our Campaigns,* pp. 235-236, 244; Bates, *History of Pennsylvania Volunteers*, 1, p. 586; McCracken, *Pennsylvania at Gettysburg*, vol. 1, p. 248. Woodward wrote repeatedly that he gave Upjohn the flag, however, in his

CSR, Woodward named John Shalck as the person who took the flag from him. McCracken stated that members of Jackson's brigade secured the flag, perhaps someone in the 11th Reserves captured the flag and brought it to Woodward.

47. *OR* 21, p. 512; Bates, *History of Pennsylvania Volunteers*, 1, pp. 639, 670, 728, 919; Harper, *Chester County*, p. 182; Thomson and Rauch, *History of the Bucktails*, p. 234; Sypher, *Pennsylvania Reserve Corps*, p. 418; Woodward, 3rd *Pennsylvania Reserves*, p. 215; Isaac R. Pennypacker, *General Meade* (New York, 1901), p. 104; Freeman Cleaves, *Meade of Gettysburg* (Norman, 1960), p. 91; George Meade, *Life and Letters of George Gordon Meade*, 2 vols. (New York, 1913), vol. 1, p. 338; Bache, *Meade*, p. 240. Meade rode a government mount instead of one of his own horses, Blacky or Baldy. Writing to his wife, Meade thought the horse was wounded on December 14 when a sharpshooter took deliberate aim at him. Bache stated that the horse was wounded at the time of the fighting.

48. Report of the Joint Committee on the Conduct of the War (Washington, 1863), Part 1, pp. 693, 705; Pennypacker, *General Meade*, p. 103; Frederick L. Hitchcock, *War From the Inside, or Personal Experiences, Impressions and Reminiscences of One of our Boys in the War of the Rebellion* (Philadelphia, 1904), p. 134.

49. Gearhart, *Spur*, 7, no. 1, pp. 16-17; Warren, *Two Reunions*, p. 18; Bates, *History of Pennsylvania Volunteers*, 1, p. 851; Alexander, *Sun*, November 3, 1895.

50. *Philadelphia Inquirer,* December 25, 1862; Woodward, 3rd *Pennsylvania Reserves*, pp. 209, 218; Bates, *History of Pennsylvania Volunteers*, 1, pp. 586, 615.

51. *OR* 21, p. 520; Woodward, *Our Campaigns*, p. 237; Bates, *History of Pennsylvania Volunteers*, 1, pp. 615, 791.

52. Thomson and Rauch, *History of the Bucktails*, p. 236; *121st Pennsylvania Survivors*, p. 38; Harper, *Chester County*, pp. 182-183; Wilson, *Alexander*, p. 119.

53. Committee on the Conduct of the War, 1, p. 693; Cleaves, *Meade of Gettysburg*, p. 92; Thomson and Rauch, *History of the Bucktails*, p. 236; Bache, *Meade*, p. 240; *OR* 21, pp. 139-140; Wilson, *Alexander*, p. 122.

54. Bates, *History of Pennsylvania Volunteers*, 1, p. 586; ibid., 4, p. 31; Gearhart, *Spur*, 7, no. 1, p. 17; Furst diary, USAMHI.

55. Taggert diary, USAMHI; Woodward, *Our Campaigns*, p. 246; John B. Tobias, "Army Life of John B. Tobias," possession of Richard Wherley, copy in FRSP; Woodward, 3rd *Pennsylvania Reserves*, p. 214.

56. *121st Pennsylvania*, p. 28.

57. Meade, *Life and Letters*, 1, p. 340.

The Death of Brig. Gen. Thomas R. R. Cobb

David L. Preston

Brigadier General Thomas R. R. Cobb was mortally wounded while directing his brigade in the defense of the Sunken Road during the Battle of Fredericksburg on December 13, 1862. Ambiguity still clouds the circumstances of the general's death. Accounts differ on how, where, and when he was mortally wounded, the nature of his wound, and where he was taken after he was struck down. These discrepancies are further muddled by postwar myths, hagiography, vilification, and casually inaccurate historical works. What really happened to General Cobb at Fredericksburg? Fortunately a large expanse of primary source material survives from which to analyze the circumstances of Thomas Cobb's death. A close study of this material allows for a clear and conclusive picture of the events of December 13.

During a short lull between the assaults of Maj. Gen. William H. French's and Maj. Gen. Winfield Scott Hancock's Federal divisions against Marye's Heights, Cobb was standing in the yard of his headquarters at the Stevens House with a group of officers. As Federal artillery from the edge of town increased its fire on the Marye's Heights area in preparation for Hancock's assault, an errant yet fatal shell passed through the Stevens House and exploded on the far side. Cobb, mortally wounded in the thigh by shrapnel from this explosion, was transported along the Sunken Road and placed in an ambulance on the Telegraph Road. All medical efforts to stop the heavy loss of blood from his severed femoral artery were unsuccessful, and he bled to death in Gen. Lafayette McLaws' divisional hospital behind Telegraph Hill.

Born in Georgia on April 10, 1823, Tom Cobb had been successful at virtually everything he attempted. Upon receiving his law degree from the University of Georgia and his admission to the bar in 1842, Cobb quickly gained prominence in Georgia and the South as an able constitutional lawyer. His most prodigious works as a lawyer were a comprehensive digest of Georgia's state laws (1851) and *An Inquiry into the Law of Negro Slavery* (1858), which included a treatise entitled *A Historical Sketch of Slavery from the Earliest Periods*. As historian Robert K. Krick notes, the latter work "combined three of Cobb's primary interests: the law, the defense of the institution of slavery, and a fervent religious endeavor."[1]

Cobb was extremely influential in Georgia's move for secession from the Union. He was elected as a delegate not only to Georgia's secession convention in 1861 but also to the Montgomery, Alabama, convention in February 1861, which oversaw the formation of the Confederate States of America. As a representative of Georgia at the Montgomery Convention, Cobb applied his expertise on constitutional law to the drafting of a provisional constitution for the new nation. He quickly grew weary of politics and decided to pursue a military career, although his work as a Confederate Congressman had been successful.[2]

Removing himself from the Confederate government in the summer of 1861, Cobb secured a colonel's commission and raised "Cobb's Legion." The Legion joined the Confederate Army in Virginia in August 1861. Its involvement in the subsequent Peninsula Campaign was minimal, and it saw no real combat. With the Legion's cavalry, Cobb participated in a number of raids with Gen. J. E. B. Stuart. Although Stuart complimented the Georgian's performance and even recommended him for higher rank, Cobb wrote to his wife that "I was left to do all the dirty work while his old West Point friends (the two Lees) [Fitzhugh and William H. F. Lee] were assigned every desirable position along the route."[3] The disaffected Cobb obtained a furlough and returned to Georgia in August 1862. He rejoined the Legion—which had been assigned to a brigade—on September 24 near Winchester, Virginia, shortly after the Battle of Sharpsburg.[4]

Throughout his service in the Army of Northern Virginia, Cobb consistently battled with his superiors. Perhaps because of his inexperience with military life, he developed an intense animosity toward professional officers, most of whom had graduated from West Point. He believed that they "not only pushed regular tactics to a ridiculous extreme, but always showed such great contempt for everybody and everything that did not savor it."[5] Cobb also expressed resentment toward his superiors over attempts to separate the cavalry and artillery from his Legion.

The fact that both he and his brother Howell's promotions were late in coming served to confirm Cobb's suspicions that the professional officers and

Brig. Gen. Thomas R. R. Cobb
(*Generals in Gray*)

members of the Confederate government in Richmond disliked him. Cobb believed that he had political enemies in the government and that professional officers looked down on him for his lack of military training. Many of his letters therefore vilify Jefferson Davis, Alexander Stephens, Judah Benjamin, and Robert E. Lee.[6] Cobb finally received his wish, however, and was appointed brigadier general on November 1, 1862, and given command of the brigade that formerly belonged to his brother. A great measure of the Georgian's gratitude should have gone to Robert E. Lee, who recommended him for the higher rank.[7] This promotion, coupled with the prospects of a transfer of his Legion to Georgia, buoyed Cobb's spirits.

He was initially skeptical of success in his efforts to get his command transferred. In a statement that had more to do with paranoia than a legitimate viewpoint, Cobb wrote that "[President Jefferson] Davis delights to thwart me so much I doubt capitally if he allows it [the transfer of Cobb's Legion], should Genl. Lee order it." In early October, however, Lee decided to send Cobb back to Georgia with the Legion. As a result, Cobb's attitude toward Lee changed immeasurably. Weeks before, he had considered Lee to be "haughty and boorish and supercilious in his bearing and is especially so towards me." After his promotion and approval of transfer of the Legion, however, Cobb conceded that General Lee was "exceedingly kind and complimentary."[8] By the time the armies had begun their march southward in November, Cobb was content that he and his men would soon be in Georgia after a quiet winter encampment near Fredericksburg, a town not unfamiliar to him. His mother's childhood home, "Federal Hill," was on the outskirts of the city, which was the destination of Lee's army.

Lieutenant General James Longstreet's Corps, to which Cobb's Brigade belonged, arrived at the outskirts of Fredericksburg on November 19 and began fortifying the heights west and south of the city. Cobb's Brigade held the right flank of McLaws' Division, which extended from Marye's Heights southward to Howison Hill. McLaws recorded that "the right brigade [Cobb's] constructed rifle-pits and breastworks of logs through the woods, with abatis in front of them."[9] William Nelson Pendleton, Lee's chief of artillery, placed a newly-arrived 30-pounder Parrott rifle near Cobb's position at Howison Hill and assigned Cobb the task of constructing earthworks and fields of fire for the artillery piece: "The work on the right and back of Mr. Howison's house was directed, with his accustomed intelligence and energy, by the since lamented General Thomas R. R. Cobb." [10]

These fortifications were no doubt impressive. In a letter to his wife, Cobb wrote, "I think my Brigade can whip ten thousand of them attacking us in the front. We have a magnificent position, the best perhaps on the line."[11] In late November and early December, Cobb's Georgians were assigned to picket duty in Fredericksburg. Cobb probably envisioned a quiet winter of picketing along the Rappahannock, for he did not believe, as his letters attest, that a battle was imminent. Three days before the battle he wrote to Marion, "I do not anticipate a battle at this place for at least some time."[12]

The following day, however, elements of the Army of the Potomac, now under the command of the recently-appointed Maj. Gen. Ambrose E. Burnside, attempted to construct pontoon bridges across the Rappahannock. The Confederates, of course, knew that the Army of the Potomac was camped across the Rappahanock. "We hear their drums and bands plainly," Cobb wrote in a letter to Marion, "and my blood boils whenever I hear them." Brigadier General William Barksdale's Mississippians, who were posted in the town, frustrated Federal efforts to bridge the river. Their tenacious resistance led the Northerners to bombard Fredericksburg on December 11. If the sound of Yankee bands infuriated Cobb, the plight of refugees and the shelling of the historic city greatly intensified his hatred of the enemy. Weeks earlier, when Cobb had heard about Union threats to shell the city, he sent a message to General Lee suggesting that Lee "ought to raise the black flag and give no quarter to any scoundrel that crosses the river."[13]

Cobb's brigade first occupied the position behind what would become known as the Stone Wall on the night of December 11, when it relieved Barksdale's Brigade, which had withdrawn to that position after combating Federals in the streets.[14] The Union assaults against Marye's Heights and Cobb's Brigade began around noon on December 13. Along his lines, Cobb encouraged his men as he awaited the first attack. According to one eyewitness: "Our brave & beloved Genl Cobb. . .pulled off his hat & waving it over his head exclaimed 'Get ready boys here they come' & they did come sure."[15]

From the Confederates' perspective, it appeared as though the Union attack would reach the stone wall. Longstreet sent word to Cobb to fall back should Richard Anderson's Division not be able to hold its position on Cobb's left flank. Cobb's alleged response to Longstreet's order was "well, if they wait for me to fall back, they will wait a long time!" General Lee confirmed that Cobb had responded to the order when he wrote that "he [Cobb] announced his determination of himself and his men to never leave their post until the enemy was beaten."[16] Cobb also sent a courier to McLaws requesting that additional reinforcements and ammunition supplies be brought up.[17] Sometime during the first assault on this position, which was being delivered by Brig. Gen. Nathan Kimball's brigade, Confederate Brig. Gen. Robert Ransom, Jr. ordered Brig. Gen. John Rogers Cooke to occupy the crest of Willis' and Marye's Hill in response to Cobb's request for reinforcements.[18] Cooke's Brigade advanced in line of battle and halted at the crest. The 27th North Carolina, however, continued down to the Sunken Road, reinforcing the 18th Georgia on the right of Cobb's line. The Washington Artillery, together with the brigades of Cobb and Cooke, proceeded to decimate Brig. Gen. Nathan Kimball's ranks in the fields below.[19] Subsequent Federal assaults by French's two remaining brigades, Cols. John W. Andrews and Oliver H. Palmer, also failed; French's division lay shattered in the open fields between the stone wall and Fredericksburg.

Colonel Palmer's brigade virtually disintegrated in the face of the overwhelming firepower brought to bear against it, and the Federals scrambled for protection. French, sensing an imminent counterattack, requested that artillery be brought up to support him.[20] Union batteries quickly advanced to the edge of town and established firing positions on Kenmore Ridge. During the short lull that elapsed between French's disastrous piecemeal assaults and Hancock's attempt, Federal artillery on Kenmore Ridge shelled the Marye's Heights area to silence Confederate guns and soften Cobb's position.[21]

Meanwhile, Confederate reinforcements advanced to the aid of Cobb's Brigade. During Andrews' attack, the 46th North Carolina went down the hill to take position in the Sunken Road behind the 24th Georgia Regiment. Brigadier General Joseph B. Kershaw's Brigade was also moving forward at this time. While Cobb's men endured enemy cannon fire and sharpshooters, Cobb stood outside the Stevens House in conference with other officers. The fatal moment for Cobb arrived during this brief interlude between Union attacks.[22]

Two theories on Cobb's death are worthy of analysis, both of which can be supported from contemporary sources. While most accounts maintain that shrapnel from an exploding artillery shell mortally wounded the general, others contend that a Federal sharpshooter was responsible for the Georgian's death. It is at least plausible that a sharpshooter ended Cobb's life, as there were Federals posted in the Stratton house, the Sisson store, and other buildings near the Confederate line.[23]

In fact, many of Cobb's superiors and contemporaries believed that a Union sharpshooter caused his death. Joseph B. Kershaw noted in his official report the difficulties he had with Federals posted in nearby buildings:"Our chief loss after getting into position in the road was from the fire of sharp-shooters, who occu-

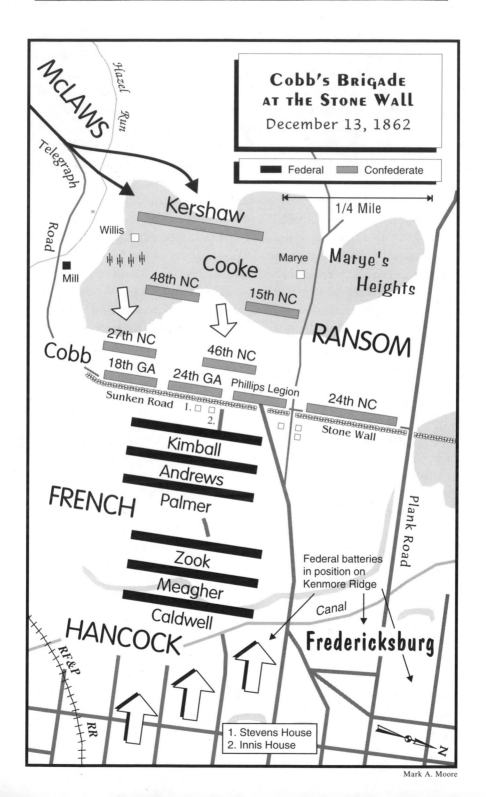

McLAWS

Hazel Run

Telegraph

Road

Cobb's Brigade at the Stone Wall

December 13, 1862

Federal   Confederate

1/4 Mile

Kershaw

Willis

Mill

Marye

Marye's Heights

Cooke

48th NC

15th NC

RANSOM

27th NC

46th NC

Cobb

18th GA

24th GA

Phillips Legion

24th NC

Sunken Road   1.
           2.

Stone Wall

Kimball

Andrews

FRENCH   Palmer

Zook

Federal batteries in position on Kenmore Ridge

Plank Road

Meagher

Caldwell

HANCOCK

RF&P

Canal

Fredericksburg

RR

1. Stevens House
2. Innis House

N

Mark A. Moore

pied some buildings on my left flank. . . .General Cobb, I learn, was killed by a shot from that quarter."[24]

In their post-war accounts, both Edward P. Alexander and Lafayette McLaws confirmed what Kershaw had written. Perhaps Cobb's fellow officers recorded only what they had been told during the battle, but they also corresponded with Kershaw and other Confederates after the war.[25] McLaws stated on the authority of Surgeon George Todd of Cobb's Brigade, who allegedly saw the wound, that Cobb was "wounded by a musketball."[26] According to Alexander, "a ball from a sharpshooter mortally wounded the gallant and Christian patriot."[27] While other veterans recollected after the war that Cobb had been killed by a sharpshooter, it is significant to note that with the exception of Kershaw's report, no contemporary source supports this. The widespread belief in secondary literature that Cobb was killed by a sharpshooter can be attributed to Douglas Southall Freeman and other writers who readily believed Kershaw's report when evaluating the circumstances surrounding his death.[28]

The most convincing evidence available, however, conclusively indicates that Cobb was wounded by shrapnel from a shell that passed through the Stevens House and exploded on the Sunken Road side of the structure. The earliest accounts of the battle all state that an exploding shell killed Cobb. Newspapers that appeared only days after the battle affirmed that a shell was the cause of the general's death. Particularly specific was the Richmond *Enquirer* report of December 13, 1862:

> A group of officers [including] Gen. Cobb. . .were standing in the telegraph road, near the scene of the action, when a shell exploded in their midst, a piece of which struck Gen. Cobb on the thigh.[29]

Many soldiers who fought at the stone wall mentioned a shell wounding Cobb. Charles J. McDonald Connaway in Company A of Cobb's Legion recorded in his diary on December 13 that "Cobb [was] killed by a peace [sic] of bomb."[30] William Montgomery of the Phillips Legion wrote to his aunt on December 17 that "a shot from the enemy's cannon gave him his mortal wound."[31]

By far the best and most accurate account of Cobb's wounding and death is by Joseph Henry Lumpkin, Cobb's father-in-law. The accuracy of his letter can be attributed to the Reverend R. K. Porter and Capt. John Cobb Rutherford, the latter a cousin of and aide to the general. These men, both eyewitnesses, accom-

panied Cobb's body back to Georgia and informed Lumpkin of what had tran-
spired. Lumpkin's letter to Callie Lumpkin details the particulars of Cobb's
wounding and death:

> A random cannon shot was fired at the House behind which
> he was standing. . . .A piece of the shell [grazed] the right
> thigh and struck the left where it lodged, breaking the bone
> and severing the femoral artery.[32]

Lumpkin wrote that the shell "entered the house on the Fredericksburg side
penetrated both rooms and exploded just as it came out of the building on the
side where he was standing." W. M. Crumley, a courier for Kershaw during the
battle, also affirmed that Cobb was "wounded by a missile from a shell, which
tore through the lower panel of the front door." During a 1900 visit to the
battlefield, he claimed to have seen this battered door hanging in the Stevens
House. When the Stevens House burned in April 1913, a local Fredericksburg
newspaper observed that the house had "a great many bullet holes in it and
many places showed where cannon balls had struck."[33]

Given that the Stevens House was Cobb's headquarters during the battle, it
is likely that he was there during the more desperate moments of the action to
receive and transmit orders. It is well documented that Cobb and a group of
officers were standing in the yard of the house when Cobb was wounded. The
officers consisted of Cobb, Brig. Gen. John Rogers Cooke, two junior officers
on Cobb's staff, and Capt. Henry A. Butler, assistant adjutant general to
Cooke.[34] The two members of Cobb's staff present were Capt. Walter Brewster,
assistant inspector general, and Capt. John McPherson Berrien, an ordnance
officer.[35] It is not conclusively known what these officers were discussing just
prior to Cobb's wounding. The presence of General Cooke and Captain Butler
suggests that the group may have discussed the positioning of Cooke's North
Carolina regiments, which had arrived to reinforce Cobb's line. Minutes before
Cobb was wounded, though, a bullet struck Cooke in the head, fracturing his
skull. Cooke was taken down the Sunken Road out of danger, where an ambulance transported him to the home of a Mrs. French in the rear of Telegraph
[Lee's] Hill.[36] Little did Cobb know that he would soon follow the same route,
for a few minutes later a deadly shell exploded in the group's midst, killing
Captain Brewster and mortally wounding Cobb and Captain Berrien.

It was probably evident to Cobb that his wound was mortal, for his thigh
bone had been shattered by the shrapnel and blood gushed from a lacerated

femoral artery. Captain John Cobb Rutherford, the general's cousin and aide, was the first to reach him. The wounded general calmly asked for a tourniquet and Rutherford assisted in applying it, though the general still continued to lose blood. Rutherford sent word to Dr. E. J. Eldridge, the surgeon of Cobb's Brigade, that the general was seriously wounded. Rutherford ran into Rev. R. K. Porter, the brigade chaplain and Cobb's quarters-mate, and they returned to aid the general. Eldridge attempted to treat Cobb's wound where he lay, but it soon became apparent that even a tourniquet could not stop the effusion of blood, and stretcher bearers were brought forward.[37]

Tom Cobb, though wounded and rapidly slipping into shock, shouted words of encouragement to his men. William Montgomery of Phillips Legion wrote to his aunt a few days afterward, "I shall never forget his last look as they laid him on the litter to bear him from the field. His last words to his men were —'I am only wounded, boys, hold your ground like brave men.'"[38] The stretcher bearers transported Cobb along the stone wall, passing by the 24th and 18th Georgia Regiments. Eldridge, Porter, and Rutherford accompanied him. By this time the field in front of the wall was teeming with advancing Federals from Hancock's Division, and an intense enemy fire was focused on the defenders of Marye's Heights. One veteran from the 24th Georgia later recalled that "the fire was so heavy that they laid him [Cobb] down and sheltered themselves under the wall for a little time. . . ."[39]

Once the party had passed around the base of Willis' Hill and reached relative safety, the bearers transferred Cobb to an ambulance on the Telegraph Road that transported him to a hospital in the rear of the army.[40] In her diary entry for December 13, Jane Howison Beale noted that Cobb was taken to "Mrs. Wiet's" house behind Telegraph Hill. That house, along with "Mrs. Goodwin's" house directly across the Telegraph Road, functioned as McLaws' divisional hospital. The sight of "Ambulances of wounded men. . .piles of amputated limbs already collecting in the corners of the yards" greeted the ambulance bearing Cobb and his aides. Thomas Cobb continued to lose blood and asked for someone to tighten his tourniquet. Although the suffering Georgian was treated by Eldridge and Dr. John T. Gilmore, chief surgeon of McLaws' Division, the damage to his thigh proved too severe, however, and the surgeons could not save his life. As Reverend Porter cradled Cobb's head in his arms, the general cried out repeatedly, "Porter, it is very painful!" He soon faded into unconsciousness, and around 2:00 p.m. on the afternoon on December 13, 1862, as Porter later eulogized, "the glorious light went out forever." Tom Cobb was dead.[41]

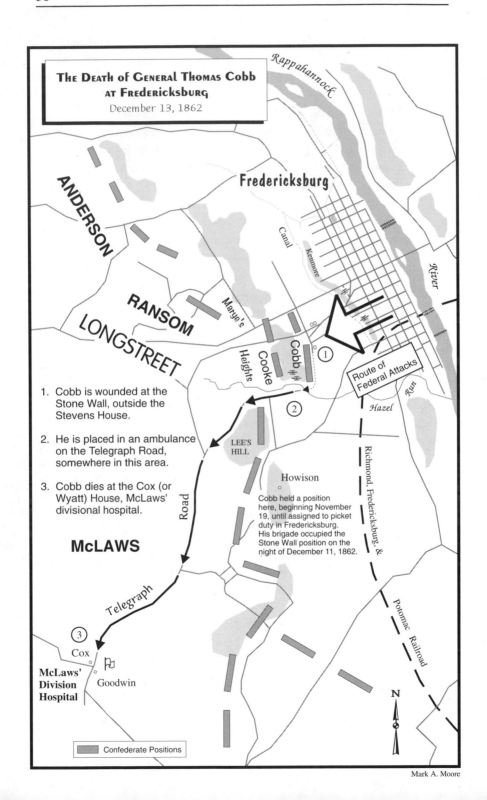

The Death of General Thomas Cobb at Fredericksburg

December 13, 1862

1. Cobb is wounded at the Stone Wall, outside the Stevens House.

2. He is placed in an ambulance on the Telegraph Road, somewhere in this area.

3. Cobb dies at the Cox (or Wyatt) House, McLaws' divisional hospital.

McLAWS

Cobb held a position here, beginning November 19, until assigned to picket duty in Fredericksburg. His brigade occupied the Stone Wall position on the night of December 11, 1862.

Route of Federal Attacks

Confederate Positions

Mark A. Moore

Back along the Sunken Road, Cobb's regiments, with the help of Cooke's and Kershaw's brigades, successfully defended the line against repeated enemy assaults. At the conclusion of the battle, Reverend Porter "carried the body to our camp, and there had it dressed for burial." Evidently some of Cobb's troops came to pay their last respects to their commander in camp. John W. Clark, a courier in Cobb's Brigade, recollected that upon returning to camp, "I saw my dear general dead, covered with a battle flag." Porter, Rutherford, two of Cobb's brothers-in-law, and Cobb's black servant accompanied his body to Richmond, and thence to Athens, Georgia, where he was buried on December 19 at Oconee Hill Cemetery.[42]

As one who gave his life for the Confederacy, General Cobb has long been the object of heroic praise by postwar Southern historians and writers. His reputation as a military commander, however, is founded almost exclusively on his role at Fredericksburg, where he defended a virtually impregnable position. It is unknown, of course, how Cobb's reputation as a military leader would have developed had he lived. Many in the Army of Northern Virginia recognized him as having merit and favored his promotion to brigadier (e.g. Stuart, Pendleton, McLaws, and Barksdale). As noted earlier, Robert E. Lee recommended Cobb for his promotion.[43]

Cobb's contribution to the victory at Fredericksburg was a substantial one, and he demonstrated a common sense that served him and the Confederates well. He stubbornly held the Confederate left against repeated attacks after he had received orders to fall back if Anderson was unable to hold his position. Cobb also asked for more reinforcements to be brought up, which solidified the Southern line against the most powerful Union attacks. Had he been less tenacious and retreated to the top of the heights, the battle might have progressed in a substantially different manner. In the end, Cobb's death produced an outpouring of sorrow, eulogies, and kind words for the departed general. The sense of loss expressed by Cobb's men, his fellow officers, and the Confederacy bear witness to his worth not only as an individual, but also as a talented officer who sacrificed his life for the Southern cause.

APPENDIX A

"The 'Federal Hill' Myth"

A number of legends arose after the war concerning Cobb's death. One of the boldest assertions concerning Cobb's death appeared in an issue of a Georgia newspaper just after the turn of the century. The article detailed an interview with a veteran of the Phillips Legion who claimed that a comrade of his murdered Cobb during the Battle of Fredericksburg. This account is refuted, however, by eyewitness accounts of Cobb's death and by the large numbers of letters written by Cobb's men which testify to their liking for Cobb and their sadness over his death.[44] The most common legend is that a Northern battery placed in the yard of "Federal Hill" fired the projectile that mortally wounded Cobb. It was widely known after the battle that "Federal Hill" was Cobb's mother's childhood home.[45] Indeed, Cobb wrote to his wife to "tell ma my camp is now on the hills immediately in the rear and west of old 'Federal Hill.'"[46] After the war, this well-known fact was weaved into the story of the general's death and evolved into an elaborate myth. By 1900 the myth had become so accepted that an article in the *Southern Historical Society Papers* claimed that "General Cobb was struck by a shot fired from a gun in the yard of 'Federal Hill,' placed, it was said, beneath the windows of the very room in which his mother was married."[47]

The occurrence is not outside the realm of possibility, as Union batteries came to Kenmore Ridge late during French's assault and fired on Marye's Heights and the stone wall. A section of Capt. William A. Arnold's Battery (A), 1st Rhode Island Light Artillery, may have been near Federal Hill. As Thomas Aldrich, a veteran of Arnold's battery, later recalled:

> [We] started directly up through the centre of the city, to the outlying houses, where we went into battery by sections into different yards, the right section being just to the left of Hanover Street in the yard of a brick mansion.[48]

Arnold recorded in his official report that the section had been placed "in the back part of the city, between two houses," with orders to "fire on the rifle-pits of the enemy."[49]

Despite its anecdotal appeal, there is no contemporary evidence to substantiate the claim that an artillery piece depolyed on 'Federal Hill' fired the fatal shot. It would have been difficult during the fighting to know with anything approaching certainty the origin of a particular shell. In addition, the well-known fact that Cobb's mother lived at Federal Hill suggests that local tradition, rather than hard evidence, was the source of the myth. The Federal Hill myth also fits with the Southern postwar tendency to view the South's defeat as something that was destined to occur. Thus the coincidence of Cobb's mortal wound coming from an artillery shell fired from his mother's home suggests the intervention of fate in a potent and ironic way. There is simply no basis of truth in the Federal Hill legend.

APPENDIX B

Lt. Col. Robert T. Cook or
Brig. Gen. John Rogers Cooke?

Many primary and most secondary sources assume that Brig. Gen. John Rogers Cooke, who was wounded during the battle, was with Cobb on the Sunken Road. The evidence for this presumption, however, is far from conclusive. Oddly enough, there are no extant accounts from soldiers in either Phillips Legion or the 24th Georgia that mention the presence of John Rogers Cooke at the Stevens House prior to Cobb's wounding. In addition, many newspapers and letters inaccurately reported that General Cooke was killed during the fighting, when in fact he survived the war. Furthermore, Cooke was wounded by a bullet, not shrapnel. While evidence does point to John Rogers Cooke's presence in the Sunken Road, there is a substantial body of evidence, perhaps more convincing, that the "Cooke" who was with Cobb was actually Lt. Col. Robert T. Cook, the commanding officer of Phillips Legion. The question has not been definitively settled.[50]

The best evidence that John Rogers Cooke was with Cobb is from Capt. Henry A. Butler, his adjutant. Butler wrote to the *Confederate Veteran* in 1906 that Cooke, talking to Cobb near the Stevens House, had been wounded minutes before the fatal shell exploded. Newspapers often added "Gen. Cook of N.C." as well, which indicates they knew exactly who was with Cobb.[51]

Conversely, William R. Montgomery of Phillips Legion noted on December 17, 1862, "our beloved Col. Cook was killed before the engagement was fairly commenced" (which holds true for Cobb as well).[52] Stephen Dent, a courier for Cobb on December 13, claims that he had delivered a message to General Cooke on Marye's Heights telling him to bring his brigade forward. After conveying his message, Dent arrived back at Cobb's line minutes after Cobb had been mortally wounded. The courier writes that "General [John Rogers] Cooke could not have been wounded from this shell, as he was charging to the relief of the Eighteenth [Georgia] on the extreme right of the brigade line."[53] Perhaps most convincing is an obituary that appeared shortly after the battle in a Georgia newspaper which reported that "he [R. T. Cook] fell, as he had stood, side by side with the gallant Tom Cobb."[54]

An alternative explanation for the confusion over Colonel Cook and General Cooke is that soldiers and correspondents simply confused their names. They heard not only that a high ranking officer named "Cook" (Lt. Col.) had been killed at the Sunken Road with Cobb, but also that Gen. John Rogers Cooke had been seriously wounded. They merely assumed Colonel Cook to be General Cooke, whose brigade had been at the Stone Wall or on Marye's Heights behind Cobb's men.

Endnotes:

1. Robert K. Krick, "Thomas Reade Rootes Cobb," in William C. Davis, ed., *The Confederate General*, six vols., (Harrisburg, 1991), vol. 2, p. 2.

2. William B. McCash, *Thomas R. R. Cobb: The Making of a Southern Nationalist* (Macon, 1983), pp. 187-190, 200-201, 209-220.

3. Ibid., pp. 248, 252, 301, 304-307.

4. The Legion was assigned to Brig. Gen. Howell Cobb's Brigade, Thomas' brother.

5. Thomas Reade Rootes Cobb Collection, University of Georgia, Athens, Georgia, T. R. R. Cobb December 9, 1862 letter to Marion Cobb.

6. McCash, *Cobb*, pp. 283-85, 303.

7. U.S. War Department, War of the Rebellion: *A Compilation of the Official Records of the Union and Confederate Armies*, 128 vols. (Washington, D.C., 1880-1901), vol. 19, p. 683. Hereinafter cited as *OR*; Krick, "Thomas R. R. Cobb," p. 3.

8. McCash, *Cobb*, pp. 306, 312.

9. *OR* 21, p. 578.

10. Ibid., p. 564. Cobb wrote to his wife Marion on December 2, 1862, that "General Pendleton visited my works today and was so well pleased that he promised to send me a large thirty pound Parrot gun to place in my fort."

11. T. R. R. Cobb Collection, Thomas R. R. Cobb November 22, 1862 letter.

12. McCash, *Cobb*, pp. 314-316; T. R. R. Cobb Collection, Thomas R. R. Cobb December 10, 1862 letter.

13. T. R. R. Cobb Collection, Thomas R. R. Cobb November 22, 1862 letter.

14. *OR* 21, pp. 578-580.

15. William R. Montgomery Letters, University of South Carolina, Columbia, South Carolina, William R. Montgomery [Phillips Legion] December 17, 1862 letter.

16. Robert Underwood Johnson and Clarence Clough Buel, eds., *Battles and Leaders of the Civil War*, 4 vols. (New York, 1884-1889), vol. 3, William Miller Owen, "A Hot Day on Marye's Heights," pp. 97-99; *OR* 21, p. 1067-1068.

17. Lafayette McLaws, "The Confederate Left at Fredericksburg," *B & L*, 3, pp. 91-92.

18. *OR* 21, p. 625. Joseph B. Kershaw also sent reinforcements in response to Cobb's pleas for assistance. Ibid., p. 588. Kimball's brigade was part of William H. French's Federal division.

19. Ibid., pp. 629-630.

20. Ibid., p. 287.

21. It is more likely that these guns, rather than Stafford Heights artillery, fired on Marye's Heights before Hancock's attack. The close proximity of Union troops to the Sunken Road argues against the use of artillery across the river, unless it was deliberately overshooting the Sunken Road to hit Confederate reserves. See Appendix A, "The 'Federal Hill' Myth," for additional information on the specific Union batteries that advanced to Kenmore Ridge.

22. The report of Col. Robert McMillan, who assumed command of Cobb's Brigade after Cobb was wounded, stands in sharp contrast to virtually all other accounts dealing with the timing of Cobb's wounding. The vast majority of these accounts maintain that Cobb was killed after the third assault. McMillan, however, states that Cobb fell 12-15 minutes after Kimball's attack. *OR* 21, p. 609. Considering the equally and perhaps more reliable sources which state that Cobb was killed after Palmer's attack, McMillan's report can safely be discounted. It is not unreasonable to argue that his report might have been self-serving, for it suggests that he, and not Cobb, was in command at the height of the attacks against the Sunken Road.

23. See Noel G. Harrison, "Gazetteer of Historic Sites Related to the Fredericksburg and Spotsylvania National Military Park" (Fredericksburg, 1986), pp. 129-131, 138-141, for additional information on Federal sharpshooters using these buildings.

24. *OR* 21, p. 590.

25. Letter from Lafayette McLaws to Kershaw dated April 1, 1887, Joseph B. Kershaw Papers, Southern Historical Collection, University of North Carolina, Chapel Hill, North Carolina. McLaws inquires of Kershaw if he knew the circumstances of Cobb's death.

26. Lafayette McLaws, "The Confederate Left at Fredericksburg," p. 94. The surgeon McLaws referred to, George Todd, was a brother-in-law of Abraham Lincoln and surgeon of the 10th Georgia. Reverend Porter and Dr. Eldridge do not mention him in their accounts of Cobb's death at the field hospital. The possibility exists, however, that Abraham Lincoln's brother-in-law treated Cobb, an ardent secessionist.

27. Edward P. Alexander, "The Battle of Fredericksburg," *Southern Historical Society Papers*, 52 vols., vol. 10 (January-February, 1882), p. 450.

28. Douglas Southall Freeman, *Lee's Lieutenants: A Study in Command*, 3 vols. (New York, 1943), 2, p. 361. Freeman cites Kershaw's report as his main evidence, and it is likely he read E. P. Alexander's 1882 *SHSP* article as well. Freeman also cites John Goolrick's *Historic Fredericksburg* (Richmond, 1922), p. 51. See also, Shelby Foote, *The Civil War: A Narrative*, 3 vols. (New York, 1963), 2, p. 38.

29. "Particulars of the Death of Gen. Cobb," *New York Times*, December 26, 1862, quoting from Richmond Enquirer, December 13, 1862 (dateline). See also "The Conflict at Fredericksburg," *Staunton* (Va.) *Spectator*, December 16, 1862; "Additional Particulars of Saturday's Battle," *Athens* (Ga.) *Southern Watchman*, December 17, 1862. Most newspapers concurred that Cobb was wounded by a shell.

30. Diary of Charles J. McDonald Connaway, Sr., Georgia Department of Archives and History, Atlanta, Georgia, December 13, 1862.

31. William R. Montgomery Letters, William R. Montgomery December 17, 1862 letter.

32. Letter from Joseph H. Lumpkin dated December 30, 1862, to Callie Lumpkin, Lumpkin Papers, Special Collections, University of Georgia, Athens.

33. Ibid.; W. M. Crumley, "The House and Battlefield Where Gen. Cobb Was Killed," *Atlanta Journal*, April 20, 1901; "Stevens House Burns," *Fredericksburg Daily Star*, April 25, 1913.

34. It is by no means conclusive that Brig. Gen. John Rogers Cooke was with Cobb in the Sunken Road. A substantial body of evidence indicates that Lt. Col. Robert T. Cook, commanding officer of Phillips Legion, was the "Cook" that was wounded with Cobb when the fatal shell exploded. See Appendix B, "Cook or Cooke?," for a detailed investigation of this question.

35. The *Richmond Enquirer*, December 13, 1862 accurately records the identities of the officers in this group with the exception of "Gen. Cook" and "Capt. Herring." Capt.

J. M. Berrien was incorrectly identified as "Capt. Herring," although the article correctly reported that he was wounded in the hip. See Berrien's Compiled Service Record for further details.

36. H[enry]A. Butler, "Fredericksburg—Personal Reminiscences," *Confederate Veteran*, 40 vols. (April, 1906), vol. 14, p. 181.

37. Lumpkin Papers, Joseph Henry Lumpkin December 26, 1862 letter; R. K. Porter January 9, 1863 letter to Howell Cobb, in *CV* 7 (January, 1889), p. 309; Carlton-Newton-Mell Collection, University of Georgia, Athens, Georgia, E. J. Eldridge April 187[ ] letter to E. D. Newton.

38. William R. Montgomery Letters, December 17, 1862 letter.

39. E[lijah] H[enry] Sutton, *Grandpa's War Stories* (Demorest, Ga., 1910), p. 22.

40. Lumpkin Papers, Joseph Henry Lumpkin December 30, 1862 letter; Confederate Veteran, 7, p. 309; Carlton-Newton-Mell Collection, E. J. Eldridge April 187[] letter.

41. Barbara P. Willis, ed., *The Journal of Jane Howison Beale of Fredericksburg, 1850-1862* (Fredericksburg, 1979), pp. 75-76; Lumpkin Papers, Joseph Henry Lumpkin letter, December 30, 1862; Carlton-Newton-Mell Collection, Dr. E. J. Eldridge Letter, April 187[ ]; *OR* 21, p. 582; *CV* 7, p. 309.

42. Ibid.; John W. Clark, "Great God What a Costly Sacrifice," Atlanta Journal, June 8, 1901; McCash, *Cobb*, p. 321.

43. See R. K. Porter, "A Portrait of Gen. T. R. R. Cobb," *Land We Love*, vol. 3 (July, 1867), pp. 183-97, for an example of early postwar writing on Cobb.

44. *Marietta Journal*, March 21, 1901.

45. *Staunton Spectator*, December 23, 1862; R. K. Porter, *Land We Love*, 3, p. 93. Most newspapers, especially those printed in Georgia, reported this fact.

46. Letter from Thomas R. R. Cobb to Marion Cobb, dated November 22, 1862. T. R. R. Cobb Collection.

47. A. L. Hull, ed., "Thomas R. R. Cobb," *SHSP* 28 (1900), p. 301. See also L. S. Marye, "Remarkable Historical Coincidence," *Fredericksburg Daily Star*, November 15, 1911; and Goolrick, *Historic Fredericksburg*, p. 51.

48. Thomas M. Aldrich, *The History of Battery A: First Regiment Rhode Island Light Artillery in the War to Preserve the Union, 1861-1865* (Providence, 1904), p. 161. Other Federal batteries present were Capt. John D. Frank's 1st New York Light Artillery, Battery G; and Lt. Edmund Kirby's 1st U.S. Artillery, Battery I.

49. *OR* 21, pp. 266-67.

50. Douglas Southall Freeman, in *Lee's Lieutenants*, 2, p. 362, for example, argues that John Rogers Cooke was on Willis' Hill when he was wounded.

51. See H[enry] A. Butler, "Fredericksburg—Personal Reminiscences," *CV*, 14 (April, 1906), p. 181. See also "Particulars of Gen. Cobb's Death," *Athens* (Ga.) *Southern Banner*, December 24, 1862.

52. William R. Montgomery Letter, December 17, 1862, W. R. Montgomery Letters.

53. S[tephen] T. Dent, "With Cobb's Legion at Fredericksburg," *Atlanta Journal*, August 10, 1901. See also, Dent's article "With Cobb's Brigade at Fredericksburg," *CV* 22 (November, 1914), pp. 500-501. The *Atlanta Journal* report enhances Dent's trustworthiness. Cf. Dent's account on the arrival of Cooke's Brigade to the account discussed earlier in this article.

54. Henry Rootes Jackson Scrapbooks, Georgia Department of Archives and History, Atlanta (microfilm edition), "The Late Lt. Col. T. R. Cook (newspaper article)."

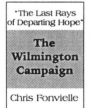

Private William McCarter and the
and the Irish Brigade at Fredericksburg

edited by Kevin E. O'Brien

Editor's Introduction:

Villiam McCarter, a young Irish immigrant, enlisted in the Union Army on August 23, 1862. When asked after the war why he volunteered, McCarter answered that he joined because of: "my love for my whole adopted country, not the North, nor the South, but the Union, one and inseparable, its form of government, its institutions, its Stars and Stripes, its noble, generous, brave, and intelligent people ever ready to welcome, and to extend the hand of friendship to the down-trodden and oppressed of every clime and people." The zealous McCarter left Philadelphia and became a private in Company A, 116th Pennsylvania Infantry, a regiment raised by Colonel Dennis Heenan, a well-known and respected commander of local militia.[1]

The 116th Pennsylvania headed for the nation's capital with many other newly-raised regiments from the North and mustered in the Army of the Potomac during early September, 1862. Spared the horrors of Antietam on September 17, 1862, McCarter and his comrades dug trenches, drilled, and learned the art of soldiering in base camps near Washington, D.C.[2] On October 6, 1862, the regiment was ordered to proceed to Harper's Ferry and join the famous Irish Brigade, commanded by Brigadier General Thomas F. Meagher, exiled Irish revolutionary and prominent New York lawyer.[3]

The Irish Brigade, officially the Second Brigade, First Division, Second Corps of the Army of the Potomac, was already the stuff of legend. Known by its distinctive emerald-green battleflags, the Irish Brigade had made a name for itself during Major General George B. McClellan's Peninsula Campaign, used as a rearguard to protect retreating Federal forces at Gaines' Mill, Savage's Station, and White Oak Swamp. The three original regiments of the Irish Brigade—the 63rd, 69th, and 88th New York—lost nearly 500 men as McClellan slogged toward the rear through Virginia swamps. "I wish that I had twenty thousand more men like yours," said General McClellan to General Meagher after the Union Army reached safety at Harrison's Landing.[4]

A few months later, Meagher's Irishmen assailed the Bloody Lane at Antietam, driving against Confederates protected by a sunken road. Cheering and waving swords and hats, the soldiers of the Irish Brigade dashed at the Rebel line, only to be met by Southern rifles flashing like a quarter-mile long bolt of lightning. Before being relieved by other Federal troops, Meagher's Irish Brigade lost 540 killed, wounded, and missing during about 15 minutes of furious combat.[5]

The veteran New York Irishmen greeted the rookies of the 116th Pennsylvania warmly, grateful for reinforcements. Lieutenant Colonel St. Clair Mulholland, second-in-command of the 116th, remembered that General Meagher himself passed around a canteen of whiskey cheer when the Pennsylvanians arrived.[6] McCarter and his regiment marched south with the New York Irish when the Fredericksburg campaign started in late October 1862. Further strengthened by the 28th Massachusetts, a predominantly Irish unit from Boston, Meagher commanded five regiments in the reconstituted Irish Brigade.

On December 13, 1862, the Irish Brigade was ordered to make a suicidal attack against the almost impregnable Confederate position on Marye's Heights at Fredericksburg. Fired up by burning, eloquent words from General Meagher, the Irishmen rushed up the hill with wild cheers. A hail of Rebel shrapnel, canister, and rifle balls swept through the lines of the five regiments, withering the ranks. The courageous charge up the bloody incline failed, but it was the high point in the Irish Brigade's illustrious career. The reckless valor of the Irish even excited the admiration of their enemy. General Robert E. Lee simply said of the Irish Brigade at Marye's Heights: "Never were men so brave."[7]

Private William McCarter dashed up the slope with his Pennsylvania comrades. Suffering multiple wounds, McCarter barely survived his ordeal on Marye's Heights. After spending five months in hospitals, he was medically discharged from the Union Army because of a severe shoulder wound.

Between 1875 and 1879, at the request of his family and friends, McCarter wrote *My Life in the Army* on his service with the 116th Pennsylvania Infantry.[8]

His memoirs on the Battle of Fredericksburg offer an intimate perspective on the experience of a combat infantryman in one of the most famous charges in American history. McCarter had a wonderful memory and an eye for detail, covering the prelude to the assault as well as the action itself. Courage, pluck, and a simple faith in God's mercy enabled him to survive the horrors of Marye's Heights.

Never before published, the following excerpts chronicle the ordeal of McCarter and the Irish Brigade on December 13, 1862. McCarter's entire manuscript is being edited for publication by Savas/Woodbury Publishers.

Waiting for the Assault:
The Morning of December 13, 1862

Sleep was unknown to the majority of my regiment during the night. Myself and a few others, however, enjoyed about two hours rest and repose alongside the mast of a ship, lying on the wharf.[9] This was not prohibited by our officers, on the contrary, they advised the men to take whatever rest they could, within certain bounds. But few did so, I suppose for the reason that the approaching struggle counteracted all such inclination except in a few cases, myself one of the latter. Although not over, probably, 1000 yards from the enemy's front, we felt pretty secure from being taken by surprise by any part of the Rebel Army, for the reason that between our position and the enemy, stood the houses of the city, and a picket line of Union troops numbering 11,500 men on the other side of the town. Consequently, had the enemy advanced out of his works upon the city, then filled with our soldiers, during the night, he would first have to drive in our picket line which certainly would have awaked any slumberers like myself and a few of my companions. Under such a feeling of security then, from at least sudden danger, a few of the boys had a short nap on the cold ground.

At a little after four o'clock I was awoke by the loud talk of some of our men close by, standing near the edge of the wharf watching Rebel shells bursting and falling in the river. I quickly jumped up, rubbed my eyes and joined the boys. These shells, flying over our heads, evidently intended to take effect upon that part of our artillerymen yet on Stafford Heights, but falling far short of their intended destination, burst over the middle of the river, or near it, and falling into the water, were harmless. The Rebel gunners had either lost our range, or were firing too high, for the shells thrown took no effect anywhere among our troops. In about half an hour, their fire ceased, till long after morning's dawn—this, however, was only "the calm before the storm."

At or about six o'clock, several officers of our regiment visited their men busily engaged cooking breakfast at the various fires here and there on the ground. To the question asked these officers, "When do you think that the regiment will go into action?" the reply was "Don't know," adding, "Hold yourselves ready any moment after daybreak." Breakfast over, the intervening time was spent in smoking and talking over the situation and prospects of fighting. A few minutes later, volley after volley of musketry broke in upon my ears, as if proceeding from the Confederate works on, or in the vicinity of Marye's Heights behind the town, and the very locality, as we were soon given to understand, which was to be assaulted by Hancock's entire division, (including my own regiment and brigade) numbering between five and six thousand men.[10] We soon learned that the firing now going on was between the Confederates on the heights just named, and General French's whole division of our army, which was to have the honor of first assaulting this distinguished Rebel stronghold, and in the event of the attack not proving successful, another was to be immediately made by the veteran troops of Hancock.

French's Division is now engaged in real earnest.[11] Thousands of muskets rattle on the morning air in one long, unceasing roll and roar of death and destruction. The smell of burning powder is almost suffocating to us in our present position, probably not within half a mile of the scene of the actual conflict. The city, and a broad tract of ground lies between us and the battlefield. The ball is now fairly opened by French and his men. Their music of death floats upon every breath of air—their countless little minie balls are singing unpleasant songs in passing the ear of many a Rebel soldier, or in causing not a few to bite the dust. Their fire ceases—why is this have they taken the coveted heights, driven the enemy out of his works, or made them prisoners of war? A few minutes more tell the tale of the terrible defeat and retreat of the gallant French with scarce the half of his men leaving the other half dead, wounded and dying on the battleground immediately in front of Marye's Heights. Sad, bitter, crushing defeat to the Union arms. But the fearful task must be tried again and that too by the invincible, desperate and unyielding Hancock and his old and well tried veterans.

By this time, the distant musketry firing had almost ceased, except a few scattering Rebel shots fired after some poor, unfortunate Union soldier fleeing for dear life from the immediate battleground. Our officers now commence to assemble within their respective regimental lines, indicative of a forward movement of my regiment brigade and division soon to be made. One of our lieutenants approaching a squad of men conversing upon the situation and the prospects of the day, was asked, "What news from the battlefield, Lieutenant?" to which he replied exactly, "Well, boys, French is licked, to beat Hell," and added in substance, "We are soon to go over the same ground and try the same job that he failed to accomplish. We expect the order momentarily to move out to the assault—Be ready, Be firm—Keep cool and do your duty when brought face to face with the enemy."

This news, although discouraging, was by no means unexpected so far as the defeat of this part of our army was concerned, for we had good reason to believe that French's Division had met with not only a terrible repulse, but that the Confederates had gained a great victory over them. In our then low position near the river we could not see the contending forces, but distinctly heard the wild, taunting cheers and yells of the foe in his works as he poured his deadly rain of bullets, grape and canister into the faces of the devoted body of Union soldiers, advancing into the very jaws of certain unavoidable death, falling down by tens, by scores, by thousands, leaving the fortunate survivors to be driven back in the utmost disorder, a confused, demoralized mob.

This was about 9 o'clock, and the weather which had been clear and sunny an hour before, suddenly became dark and cloudy as if mourning over the recent catastrophe to one portion of the Union Army. A few minutes later, the sound of a horse's hoofs is heard, galloping at the top of his speed down the first street running parallel with the river towards our brigade position. In another moment the horse and his rider appears at the end of a row of houses which had hidden both from our view till reaching that locality. The rider, we soon recognize to be Hancock, clad in his usual battlefield uniform, that of a private soldier, ready for the fray. In a voice like thunder he gives the order to the brigade commanders, "Fall In," then putting spurs to his fiery charger, dashes away with lightning speed, and is again lost to our view. In another moment, likewise mounted, and similarly clad, appears our own beloved, and no less brave, brigade commander, General Meagher reiterating Hancock's order, "Fall In," which is at once taken up by each officer who in turn telegraphs the long looked and wished for summons throughout the entire brigade, in a moment of time. That "Fall In" was the "death-knell" to many a brave and loyal heart in the Irish Brigade of the Army of the Potomac, on that ever memorable, dark 13th of December, 1862. But the order was quickly and willingly responded to with an alacrity never equaled by the same troops on any previous or similar occasion, each man seeming to thoroughly realize his own individual responsibility as a soldier in retrieving the terrible defeat and repulse of French not quite an hour before. The troops were soon in line, and with loaded muskets, anxiously awaited further orders. Just then, General Meagher again appears on horseback, at the end of the row of houses already mentioned. The orderlies are about him, bearing in their arms large bunches of green boxwood. The general, then, did not come nearer the regiment, but sent, by the orderlies to our officers, the bunches of boxwood, requesting them to present, in his name, a green sprig to each man in the ranks, to stick in his cap, before advancing against the enemy.[12] This was something I did not at first understand, but soon found out what it meant, and that General Meagher had always been in the habit of leading his brigade into battle with at least two emblems of Erin's nationality—the "green sprig," and the "green flag," which the Rebels had frequently admitted was a terror to them, because they well knew the dogged, stubborn fighting qualities of the men who bore them.*

*McCarter's Note: "The piece, or sprig of green that was presented to myself on the above occasion or rather the remains of it, I can show today (March 20, 1878) preserved in a bottle."

The Advance Through Fredericksburg

. My regiment now filed off of the wharf at the extreme end of the town, into the first street south of it running east and west, and there joined the other regiments of the brigade, namely, the 69th New York, 28th Massachusetts, 88th New York, and 63rd New York, all infantry, which together with my own regiment constituted the force of the brigade on this occasion, nearly 1,700 men.[13] We found the regiments just named drawn up in line in the middle of the street and resting on their arms, awaiting orders to advance. These regiments were separated from each other by the streets running north and south, for, to stand in these streets for a moment, was almost certain death owing to the enemy's fire having full sweep up them. My regiment at this time was the rear of the brigade, and the 69th New York, the advance, or head. This arrangement, in disposition of the line I soon learned was made so that the position of the 116th regiment (my own) would be the extreme right, and the 69th New York the extreme left of our brigade line of battle in attacking the enemy.[14] My regiment after reaching a certain point in this street, was ordered to halt and like the others, to rest, in place, on their arms—Then followed another season of that terrible suspense and anxiety which I have elsewhere spoken of in this little narrative—And, oh, what fearful suspense—I fancy I experience it yet.

A large woolen or cotton factory stood upon one side of the street in our front. It had been set on fire by our artillery early the morning before, and its contents continued to burn amid fallen walls and broken, crushed machinery. Our position, therefore, was anything but comfortable, or safe here owing to the smoke from the burning ruins, and a high wall yet standing but threatening every moment to tumble down on the top of us—but we dare not, without orders, change our position.

The brigade remained here for perhaps half an hour, or a little longer. I had no means of ascertaining the exact time of day, nor indeed did any of the men seem to think of it. This halt, or delay in our advance, when Rebel shells were flying in all directions, and falling and bursting in every street in the town, was most trying and painful to all, and to myself in particular, much more so in every respect, than I experienced face to face with the enemy on the field of battle. While in position here, I witnessed many horrid sights, a few of which are as follows—Here and there Negro women were seen rushing out of half demolished houses, frequently with young children in their arms, and others crying and clinging to their skirts, perfectly frantic with fright. They evidently wished to escape to some place of safety outside of the town and out of the range of the falling, bursting Rebel shells, yet, at the same time, did not seem to know which way to run in their confusion. All were to be pitied, and although our troops could render them no assistance, they had our sympathy, and the little children especially who were being dragged along shoeless and barefooted over the rough street, and in front of a line of soldiers. Onc aged Negro woman in particular attracted our attention and pity. She was coming along in a terrible hurry with a large basket in her arms, and three crying youngsters holding on to her old and torn dress. Upon reaching the intersection of two of the streets, not 15 yards from where I stood, a solid Rebel shot struck her, cutting her badly literally in two, and killing her instantly. Two of the children were also killed by the same missile, and the third fatally injured.

Many of the wounded of French's Division were now being carried into the town from the battlefield, presenting to us, who were just about to go into it, fearful pictures of the horrors of war. Very shortly every house in the city, considered comparatively out of the way of Rebel shot and shell, was a hospital, yet, even in these, cannon balls frequently crashed through the roofs and windows, instantly killing some of those who were then fast dying of their wounds within them. Whilst still in position here, one poor fellow was carried past us on a window shutter, by two soldiers. His uniform indicated the rank of captain. His face was young, and deathly white. He had been hit in the leg, above the knee, by a cannon ball, which had almost torn the limb from the body, a small thready sinew only apparently holding both together. As his comrades carried him along, the lower part of the leg nearly severed from the body, hung over the edge of the board, dangling backwards and forward at every step taken by the bearers, an extremely sickening sight to those witnessing it. Some of our boys seeing this shouted to the men carrying the poor unfortunate officer, "Lay him down, and cut the leg off at once—that will ease him." No attention however was given to this, but as the men with their wounded commander reached the center of my regiment, in passing down along our line, one of the boys there seeing the situation of the sufferer, sprung out of the ranks, with pen-knife in hand, and quick as thought, cut the thread-like sinew that seemed to be the only thing that held the two parts of the leg together. This done, the limb, from the knee down, dropped on the ground, evidently much to the satisfaction and relief of its late owner, who, very faint and weak from loss of blood could only smile and nod his head as a mark or token of thankfulness and gratitude to his thoughtful and kind benefactor.

General Meagher now comes galloping down the line in front of the men. He soon reaches the end of it, turns quickly around, passes up again at railroad speed in the rear of the troops, and is soon lost to the view of my regiment. In five minutes he appears again, in the distance, at the head of the column, waving his glittering sword overhead. A moment longer, and the order to advance with fixed bayonets, is telegraphed from regiment to regiment, from officer to officer, and the brigade is in motion once more, heading up the street to the other end of the town, its route to the point to be assaulted, on Marye's Heights. The enemy evidently sees the movement, although our troops were well hidden from his view by the houses, except when crossing the streets running north and south, for no sooner were the soldiers in motion, than he opened a furious fire of artillery upon them, killing and wounding several especially at the intersections of streets. The brigade, however, by regiments about ten yards apart, marched steadily onward amid this terrible rain of fire and death, till arriving at the other end of the town, it was again ordered to halt under cover of the houses, and close to a "high brick chimney" in the rear of a mill.

Cannon balls and shells were now flying faster than ever, and dropping thick in every part of Fredericksburg, crashing through roofs, windows and walls, and in many instances setting the houses, shielding our men, on fire, and killing or wounding several soldiers in each regiment of the brigade. But here we were, halted, and dare scarcely move, except when a Rebel missile came rushing along close overhead, to which I must confess many of our boys (myself included) paid due respect in the form of a long bow or curtsy showing no desire whatever to make a closer acquaintance with the flying messenger, or to interrupt him in his course. Our position and surroundings were certainly well calculated to stagger the bravest of troops, and cause a general stampede, but such did not occur—Meagher stood, firm as a rock, at the head of the column, and the only uneasiness visible among the rank and file was, as I have already stated, when men bowed their heads to keep them out of the way of the flying cannon balls of the enemy—yet, notwithstanding this, some of them were instantly killed. At one time, on this occasion, our Lieutenant Colonel, [St. Clair Mulholland], thinking it perhaps necessary, shouted out "Steady, Men, Steady, You'll soon get forward," but not a moment after, he himself made obeisance to a solid shot in close proximity to his head, then looking along the line of soldiers, with a rather nervous smile on his countenance, shook his head as if to say, "Steady," which under such circumstances, is easier to say than to do. Almost at the same moment, a large round shell, evidently from the lighter Rebel batteries on Marye's Heights was seen "coming for us," but falling short of our line, or about 20 yards south of it, it rolled quickly down the street, without bursting, through the vacancy between two of our regiments, and very probably found a grave in the waters of the Rappahannock. This missile had scarce disappeared, when another of much larger dimensions neared us at lightning speed, probably from the heavy batteries of the enemy on the upper, or Fredericksburg Heights. It soon proved to be a "shell," and the largest one too that I ever saw, in circumference apparently as large as a flour barrel. It struck the brick chimney alluded to, very near which I stood, at the head of our regiment, knocking the chimney down on the top of a row of low frame houses, with a terrible crash, crushing all the structures to the ground. This stopped the progress of the shell, which fell on the earth, and then bursting, not a dozen yards away, wounded Colonel Heenan very severely in the hand—myself in the calf of the left leg, drawing blood quite freely—seven of my comrades, some of them slightly, and others seriously—and instantly killing Sergeant Marley of Company "B," of my regiment.[15] I paid but little attention to my own wound, although it left the ground crimson at my feet. Colonel Heenan had his hand bandaged up, and remained at his post, and the other severely wounded men were sent back to the rear, then over the river, whilst I and three of my other slightly injured comrades, kept our places in the line, and more anxious than

Pvt. William McCarter, 116th Pennsylvania Infantry, Irish Brigade
(This post war image is courtesy of the Historical Society of Pennsylvania)

ever for the word "Forward," to try our powder face to face with our strongly entrenched opponents.

Shouts were soon heard away up at the head of the line—it was the order to advance, come at last. Nearer and nearer, from regiment to regiment, till it reached my own. Every man and officer was in his place, notwithstanding the continued rain of Rebel shot and shell. "Shoulder Arms." "Forward." "Double Quick." "Now, men, steady, and do your duty." "March," and my regiment followed close upon the heels of the other regiments of the brigade also advancing on the double quick (or run) towards the Rebel works on Marye's Heights, while our artillery, which for several hours previous had been silent on Stafford Hills, now opened a furious fire over our heads, on the enemy works to cover our advance. This fire, however, seemed to make a little impression as if directed against the rocks of Gibraltar, for the Confederate artillery fire increased, and their deadly messengers were hurled against our ranks in a manner never before experienced by the oldest regiments of the brigade. From the time that the brigade was drawn up in line in the street of the town, before advancing on the Rebel works, or even seeing a Rebel soldier in these works, till it cleared the city limits on its way to the assault, its loss was reported to be 17 men killed and 26 wounded. Hot quarters, indeed.

My regiment was now on a double-quick, and turning round a corner at the end of the town, proceeded at the same speed till it reached the base of a hill in front, on the top of which, at the opening of the engagement, stood a long, white wooden fence, now prostrated by the fire of the enemy. Immediately below this fence, probably 25 feet down, was the Fredericksburg and Richmond Railroad. Arriving at the foot of this hill, the regiment halted for a few moments to rest the now almost breathless men. Here, although much nearer the enemy than before, we were well sheltered from his fire by the hill in front. Our colonel now informed us (through orderlies) that our further route lay along the top of the ground above the railroad, and close to the fence I have named—a very narrow path and a most dangerous locality, being, as it was, open and exposed to all the Rebel batteries. But there could be no buck-out, and for what reason this route was selected for the passage of the brigade to the assault, I never knew—certainly it was a fatal road to many a Union soldier upon this occasion. At the same time, Colonel Heenan notified the regiment that as the summit of the bank of each side was so narrow, not admitting of two men abreast the troops would have to break ranks in crossing, and get over singly, or as best and as rapidly as they could. This was accordingly done, but with a loss of several men killed, and three wounded—a very small loss, considering all the circumstances. After crossing, we reached a canal, probably four or five yards wide, running through a small valley and which had also to be passed. Fortunately it contained little water at the time for many of the troops waded across, while the rest passed over on a narrow corduroy bridge of five or six small trees stretched over the water, and which early the same day, cost four men their lives in its construction—over this bridge I passed myself.

The regiment, now over the canal, quickly re-formed and dressed along the base of another hill which also covered it from the Confederate fire. To our left, about 20 paces apart, stood the other regiments of the brigade, ready to spring forward with my own to the top of the hill, where the enemy in his works stood awaiting our approach and ready to give us a warm reception. To the left of the brigade, and running along the same valley, stood the brigades of Zook and Caldwell, also ready for the charge.[16] The hill in front now only intervened between Hancock's division and the enemy. It was an exciting moment, and the long lines of armed men, waiting, as with breathless anxiety for the word "Forward," was, to me, a scene never to be forgotten. Silence reigned among the rank and file, while generals, followed by orderlies, dashed up and down the lines giving their final orders to regimental commanders. All is ready. Then comes that most terrible military command. "Fix Bayonets," which was done amid the yells and cheers of the men, resounding from one end of the valley to the other, and which the enemy, most undoubtedly, must have heard. And, as the clink, clink, clink of the cold, glittering steel being placed in position, sounded down the long rows of soldiers, many of them soon to lay down their lives on the altar of their country, one could not help thinking, that war, indeed, is sad.

Well did the Irish Brigade know what this meant, and what the nature of the work was, which now lay before them, and well did the men realize, that in preparing to use their favorite weapons of war, so dreaded by the enemy, especially when accompanied by the green flag, that a fearful, bloody struggle lay before them. One poor fellow at my side and who soon afterwards was killed, remarking in his good natured, broad Irish dialect, as he placed his bayonet on the muzzle of his musket, "Damn them, that's the 'thing' to fetch the Sons of Bitches."

I find that I have omitted to mention, in their proper place, a few facts, which I will now state—while passing along the high ground close to the white fence, the terrible effects of the Rebel fire in that particular locality were sadly and painfully visible. The ground on the top of the embankment was literally covered with dead Union soldiers of French's division, shot down in their attempt to cross it. Wounded men also lay thick on the face of the bank, and along its base, close to the railroad, whither they had crawled out of the Rebel range. Whilst myself and my regiment were passing over the same ground, my companion, Sergeant John Strechabock, who afterwards lifted me off the battle-field, suddenly attracted my attention by shouting out, as he pointed down to the railroad, "Oh, look there, Bill. Look at the watermelon." We were then on a run to clear the dangerous ground, and had not a second of time to lose for the enemy was hammering away at us, from his heights. I merely glanced at the object he pointed at. It was the body of a dead soldier, face downwards, lying on the railroad, in the center of the track. He had evidently been struck on the head by a cannon ball, which cut it in two, as clean as if cut with a knife. Then I fully understood what my companion and friend meant by the "Watermelon," for the poor, unfortunate, dead soldier's head, or rather the part of it still attached to the body, presented, at our distance, from it, exactly the appearance of a large, ripe watermelon cut through the center, "red."

The Assault

The three brigades I have named, Meagher's, Zook's and Caldwell's, numbering in all about 5,800 or 6,000 men, in double line of battle were ordered to advance. With a bound, and a yell, characteristic of perhaps Irish soldiers only, they did so, determined to force their passage at all hazards with the point of the bayonet. They saw what had befallen the men of French's noble division only a short time before, and with lips closely pressed together, they were bent on revenging it, if at all possible to do so.[17] On they went, till they reached the top of the hill, and the level ground, within 200 yards of the first line of Rebel rifle pits, and a long stone wall running close along their front where a blinding fire of musketry met them in the face, and which for but a few seconds, staggered the line.[18] It soon recovered again, however, but with a loss of several men killed and many wounded, including one officer killed, and three wounded. By this, the first Rebel musketry fire upon us here, I came very near "stopping a ball" myself, for we had scarce reached the top of the hill, when a bullet cut the leather front, or peak of my cap from its fastenings, leaving it dangling by a solitary thread at my ear. But onward pushed our line, firing as it advanced. The storm of battle increases its fury, and the crash of musketry, mingled with the roar of cannon from the peaks, is terrific. To reach the "Stone Wall" was the first object in view. We certainly tried hard to do it. When a large part of the distance had been gained, to within about 50 paces of this wall, Cobb's solid brigade of Rebel infantry, said to have been then 2,400 strong, suddenly sprang up from behind it where they had been entirely concealed from our view till that moment, and pouring volley after volley into our faces at once stopped our farther advance.[19] In connection with this fire, other Rebel infantry, in long lines behind earthworks, and in rifle pits on Marye's Heights, were blazing away at us at the same time. It was simply madness to advance as far as we did, and an utter impossibility to go farther.

Up to this moment I had received no very painful wound myself, having only been struck on the left shoulder by a spent ball, not then painful, and on the left ankle by another, which caused me some uneasiness, but did not prevent the full discharge of my duty. But I was not to get off so miraculously easy, as five minutes afterwards proved.

The rattle of musketry was now deafening. Our fire against the enemy was rapid and constant, but its effect could not be seen for the stone wall in front. The Rebel fire, although perhaps not quite so rapid as ours, was decidedly much more regular and steadier, probably owing to the men being so well protected by earthworks. It was now beginning to tell fearfully among the men of my regiment, ploughing great gaps in the ranks. Every third man had fallen, and along some parts of the line, every second soldier had been killed or wounded.[20] To make matters still worse, we had lost nearly all our officers. Colonel Heenan was again severely wounded and taken off the field, also Major Bardwell, Lieutenants Willauer and Montgomery, the latter mortally, and Lieutenant Nowlen, seriously wounded. Lieutenant Colonel Mulholland fell next, and in quick succession Lieutenant McGuire shot through the shoulder and leg and Captains Smith and O'Neill, and Lieutenants Reilly and Miles, but still my regiment held its ground. My own turn came next. Bullets had been singing their little songs around my head and ears since arriving on the battle ground, piercing my uniform from head to foot, and cutting open the cartridge box by my side, yet strange to say, none of them inflicted any wound worth naming, except the two already mentioned—one on the left shoulder, and the other on the left ankle, neither of them, at the time causing inconvenience or much pain.[21]

But now, for something much more serious to myself than at any time before. I had discharged six or seven shots, I don't know which, up to this time, and into the ranks of Cobb's brigade right in our front, behind the stone wall. I was getting ready to fire again, had taken the cartridge out of my cartridge box, bitten the end off it, inserted it into the muzzle of my musket, drew the ramrod from its place, and had just raised my right arm over my head to send the

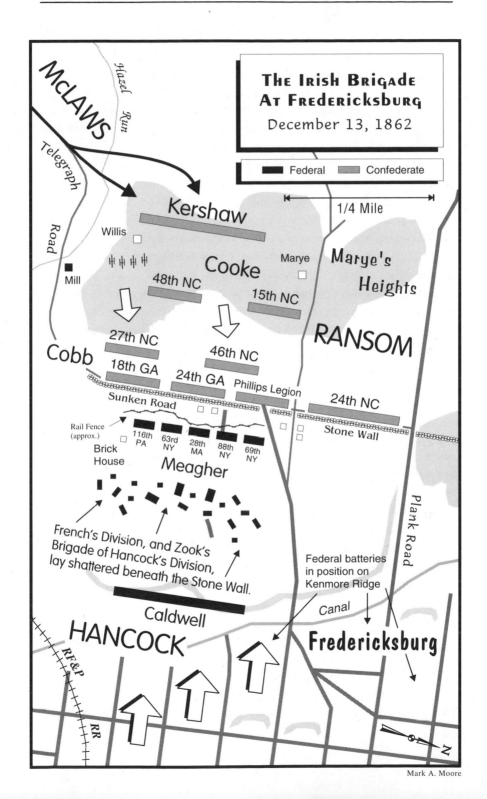

The Irish Brigade At Fredericksburg
December 13, 1862

Federal   Confederate

1/4 Mile

McLAWS

Hazel Run

Telegraph Road

Kershaw

Willis

Mill

Cooke

Marye

Marye's Heights

48th NC

15th NC

27th NC

RANSOM

Cobb

18th GA

46th NC

24th GA

Phillips Legion

24th NC

Sunken Road

Rail Fence (approx.)

Brick House

116th PA   63rd NY   28th MA   88th NY   69th NY

Stone Wall

Meagher

French's Division, and Zook's Brigade of Hancock's Division, lay shattered beneath the Stone Wall.

Federal batteries in position on Kenmore Ridge

Caldwell

Canal

Plank Road

HANCOCK

Fredericksburg

RF&P

RR

N

Mark A. Moore

cartridge home, or down into the musket, when a bullet struck me in the uplifted arm, close up to the shoulder, and the limb dropped powerless at my side. I knew something serious had happened to me, but at the moment did not realize that a Rebel bullet had hit me, inflicting a very serious wound.

At first I thought that the man in the rear, immediately behind me in the second line, or one of the men in the front, or first line, by my side, had accidently struck my elbow with a butt end of a musket, for my feelings then were exactly like those produced by being suddenly hit in that way, or by knocking my elbow a hard blow against a brick or stone wall. But in a very few seconds more I discovered what was the matter, and that I actually was shot, but in what particular spot I was yet in ignorance, although I felt it to be somewhere in the neighborhood of the shoulder. Blood flowed down the inside and outside sleeve of my uniform, then down the side of my pants into my right foot shoe, till it overflowed. Next, a dizziness in the head, and partial loss of sight came over me, accompanied by violent pain in the wounded part, and then growing very faint and weak from loss of blood, I fell down flat on my face on the ground with my musket, which I clutched with my left hand, by my side, while my comrades, now standing over me, and near me, still in line, although few indeed, continued to blaze away at the foe.

My consciousness speedily returning, I suppose by the fall, I attempted to rise and make my way to the rear, or to somewhere out of the range of the enemy's fire, but I had scarce raised my head when such a shower of bullets came around it that brought me at once to conclude that to move was dangerous and to rise up would be fatal. Accordingly, I laid down again, stretching my body out upon the earth, and lying as close to the ground as I possibly could to let the enemy's bullets pass over me. No sooner had I done this, than one of my comrades, the third man from the head, or right of the regiment, and almost my next neighbor there, was shot dead and fell about two yards in front of me, right across my body. Poor fellow, he was afterwards riddled with bullets, and owing to the position of his body, it stopped many a ball that otherwise would certainly have entered my own. As it was, bullets kept constantly whizzing over me, around me, burying themselves in the ground not a foot from my head and throwing mud and dust all over my person. My situation was truly an awful one—not more than 50 paces from a powerful, victorious foe—exposed to his three fires, left, center and right—and also in danger of the fire of all the other Union troops coming up to the attack.

In the enemy's clutches, I may almost say I lay, disabled, disheartened, hope, a mere shadow—and not knowing the moment that I might be torn to pieces by cannon ball or shell, or sent into eternity by the lesser, but just as fatal rifle ball, or musket bullet of the now taunting Confederates. I then offered up the simple but earnest prayer "Into thy hands, Oh My God, I commit my Soul and Body," after which, thank "Him," I felt more composed in my mind, and perfectly reconciled to my fate—death, or life. In another instant, another of my comrades fell, almost at my feet, mortally wounded in the stomach, exclaiming as he went down, "Oh, My Mother." He tossed about in agony and blood for a few seconds longer, then all was over—his spirit had fled.

The regiment by this time had lost close to the half of its rank and file, and nearly all of its officers, yet the men who were still unhurt, continued to blaze away at the Rebel troops behind the stone wall. The other regiments of the brigade had suffered in like proportion to my own. It was now, I suppose about 2 o'clock, and no success whatever, of any point within my own view, had crowned the Federal arms—death, havoc and carnage was visible at every step on the ground fronting Marye's Heights. I could not see now, owing to my low situation, who had command of the regiment, but distinctly heard the order given by someone in authority. "Fall back men, and everyman for himself." This was immediately done, and not a moment too soon, for ten minutes longer of such work would have resulted in the total butchery of the regiment, leaving no man in it to tell the tale. The men turned their backs on the foe, and fled in the greatest confusion towards the base of the hill which they so recently ascended to the assault, and in their retreat, the Rebel fire followed them till the low ground was reached where all now that remained of the regiment were once more comparatively out of the reach of Confederate bullets.[22]

The Aftermath

But, where was I, left all alone in my glory, if such it really was? Lying among heaps of my wounded, dying and dead companions. Cannon to my right, cannon to my left. Cannon in front, and cannon behind, vollied and thundered to the music of thousands of minie balls flying about in all directions. To rise up and run was impossible, first, because the nature of my wound would not admit of it then, and second, because had I done so, I would undoubtedly have been shot down again, and perhaps instantly killed, as it became evident, the enemy was picking off our wounded men on the battlefield, firing at them and killing them outright. To get aid, or even to expect it from any of our own men, was out of the question for no one could get near me except at the risk of their own life. So, reader, was not my position a terrible one? I must confess, that at that time, I never expected to get off, or to be taken off that bloody field alive. But it was otherwise ordered and I was spared to tell my tale.

I have spoken of the brotherly affection and attachment to each other, that existed between myself and two members of my regimental company, and to show how strong these feelings were towards myself, in the hour of battle, I must relate the following incident relating to the conduct of Lieutenant Foltz, who, to avenge my misfortune, or in trying to do so, was shot through the head and instantly killed. The incident is a follows—the survivors of the regiment had just commenced to retreat, when Lieutenant Foltz, almost at whose feet I lay on the ground, stooped down and said to me. "Bill, We've got to get—Are you badly hurt—I wish to God I could get you out of here." Before I had time to reply, some new thought or idea must have struck his mind, for he seized my loaded musket by my side, and in an unusually excited manner, moved a few yards forward, saying, "Well, I see the bastard that laid you low and I'll fetch him." Foolish man thought I—how could you "designate the man" that "shot me," among such a "multitude" of Rebel soldiers? But be this as it may, he knelt down on the ground with his left knee, placed the butt end of the musket upon the other, and took deliberate aim at something in the direction of the stone wall. I watched him closely, but ere he pulled his trigger, the musket fell out of his grasp, he nervously raised his hand to his brow, and then fell to the earth a bleeding corpse, pierced through the head by a Rebel bullet. His face was towards me, revealing the fatal wound immediately above his left eye. The profound sorrow that I then experienced, no tongue or pen could describe. There lay my late beloved, friend, and companion in his blood, almost at my side, stiff and cold and dead, and all to avenge only a wound received by myself.[23]

Immediately after my comrade [Foltz] fell, bullets were flying so thick around me, that the thought struck me to pull, or work my blankets off of my shoulder, and to place them in front of my head, as, at least, a slight protection to it from the deadly little missiles. Fortunate indeed that I thought of this, and doubly fortunate that I succeeded in doing it. The prospect of death now seemed to increase and my clothing was being literally torn from my back by the constant and furious musketry fire of the enemy from three points. A ball struck me on the left wrist inflicting another painful but not serious wound. Another, and one which would undoubtedly have proved instantly fatal but for my blankets, through six plies of which it passed, lodging in the seventh (afterwards discovered) left me the possessor of a very sore head for six weeks after. With such force did this bullet come, that for some time I really thought it had embedded itself in the skull. These blankets were the receptacles of 32 other bullets, which dropped out of them while opening them up, the next morning in Fredericksburg.

General Oliver O. Howard's division was now brought forward to the attack, supported on its left by two other divisions of the 9th Corps.[24] It was now probably three o'clock, and evidently a "general engagement" along our entire line had commenced, or very soon would do so. To my right, and to my left, as far either way as I could see, solid rows of Union soldiers were advancing up the slopes to attack the enemy. Brigade after brigade, and division after division were hurled against him time and again, but like my own, were blown back as if by the breath of hell's door suddenly opened, shattered, disordered, pell-mell down the declivities, amid the shouts and yells of a victorious foe, which made the horrid din demoniac. Howard's division which came up behind me, advanced to within about 20 yards of the place where I was lying, but were quickly stopped by the enemy's artillery on the heights, and his infantry in my front. After delivering several vollies into the Rebel lines, this division also retreated in great disorder, leaving hundreds of its numbers dead and wounded on the field. Whilst all this was going on on the lower ground, the enemy's artillery, on the Heights of Fredericksburg, and the Federal, on Stafford Heights, were rigorously firing at each other, which, with the constant rattle of at least 100,000 muskets, was deafening, and caused the ground under and around me to shake to such a degree, that at times I actually thought it was sliding away. The dead and wounded now lay very thick all around and the cries of some of the latter were heart-rendering in the extreme.

A burning thirst was now coming fast upon me—that most terrible of all thirsts known too, and experienced only by the wounded on the battlefield when water was not to be had. Oh, how I craved a cup of cold water—I would have given $1,000 for it had I had it. I would not rise from the earth, and dare not do so had I been able, for the flying bullets, to look for water, nor did I know where to find it then, nearer than the Rappahannock river, had I succeeded in getting off the battlefield with my life. A crowd of soldiers stood behind the brick house shielding them from the enemy's fire.[25] They dare not put their heads past the corner, except at the risk of their lives. I lay within 20 yards of them. I called to them, for God's sake, to throw me a canteen of water. A brave, sympathizing fellow edged out from among the crowd with canteen in hand, and crawling on hands and knees, evidently intending to get near enough to throw it to me, was struck by a bullet, causing him to beat a hasty retreat back to safer quarters, leaving me minus of the relief he so nobly tried to render, at the risk of his own life.

Darkness was now coming on, yet the conflict raged, but before 11 o'clock that night, the Army of the Potomac was a defeated, dejected and demoralized mob.

Editor's Conclusion:

Private William McCarter alternately crawled and walked down the incline of Marye's Heights after darkness fell. His friend, Sergeant Strechabock, together with another soldier from the 116th Pennsylvania, literally stumbled over McCarter after he had collapsed near the base of the hill. Strechabock and his partner carried McCarter to an ambulance.[26]

McCarter was one of the lucky living members of the Irish Brigade. Out of 1,200 men in the brigade engaged at Fredericksburg, 545 were killed, wounded, or missing, a 45% casualty rate.[27] Three of the five regimental commanders in the Irish Brigade—Maj. Joseph O'Neill of the 63rd New York, Colonel Nugent of the 69th New York, and Col. Dennis Heenan of the 116th Pennsylvania—dropped wounded.

The correspondent of Great Britain's *London Times*, who viewed the attack from behind Southern lines, wrote afterwards: "Never at Fontneoy, Albuera, or at Waterloo, was more undaunted courage displayed by the sons of Erin. The bodies which lie in dense masses within forty yards of Colonel Walton's guns are the best evidence what manner of men they were who pressed on to death with the dauntlessness of a race which has gained glory on a thousand battlefields, and never more richly deserved it than at the foot of Marye's Heights on the 13th day of December, 1862."[28]

Endnotes

1. St. Clair A. Mulholland, *The Story of the 116th Pennsylvania Regiment, Pennsylvania Infantry* (Philadelphia: F. McManus, Jr., & Company, Printers, 1903), p. 2, hereinafter cited as Mulholland, *116th Pennsylvania.*

2. Ibid., pp. 8, 9.

3. Frederick H. Dyer, *Compendium of the War of Rebellion* (Dayton, 1978), p. 1612.

4. Daniel P. Conyngham, *The Irish Brigade and Its Campaigns* (New York, 1867), p. 249.

5. United States War Department, *War of the Rebellion: A Compilation of the Official Records of the Union and Confederate Armies*, 128 vols. (Washington, D.C. 1880-1901), Series 1, vol. 19, pt. 1, p. 192. Hereinafter cited as *OR*. All citations refer to series 1.

6. Mulholland, *116th Pennsylvania*, p. 12.

7. George W. Pepper, *Under Three Flags* (Cincinnati, 1899), p. 333.

8. The original McCarter manuscript, entitled *My Life in the Army*, is on file at the Historical Society of Pennsylvania, Philadelphia, Pennsylvania.

9. McCarter was not alone in finding uncomfortable sleeping accommodations. Sergeant Peter Welsh, 28th Massachusetts of the Irish Brigade, wrote his wife that the men searched for a place to rest in ankle-deep mud. "We hunted up pieces of boards," he wrote, "and lay them down on the mud and covered ourselves up in blankets." Lawrence Kohl and Margaret Richard, ed., *Irish Green and Union Blue: The Civil War Letters of Peter Welsh, Color Sergeant, 28th Massachusetts Volunteers* (New York, 1986), p. 42, hereinafter cited as *Irish Green and Union Blue*.

10. Winfield Hancock's division numbered about 5,000 soldiers on the morning of December 13, 1862. It lost 2,021 killed, wounded, missing or captured during the assault of Marye's Heights. *OR* 21, p. 228.

11. Maj. Gen. William Henry French.

12. General Meagher ordered sprigs of evergreen placed in each man's hat to make sure that the Confederates knew they were facing the Irish Brigade. The green flags of the three New York regiments—the 63rd, 69th and 88th—had been so riddled by shot and shell that they had been returned to New York City for replacement. Only the 28th Massachusetts, which had recently received a green silk banner decorated with a golden harp, a sunburst, and a wreath of shamrocks, carried the Irish emblem into battle. The replacement symbol of green boxwood stirred the hearts of the Irish Brigade. "We all looked gay and felt in high spirits," wrote Pvt. William McCleland of the 88th New York after he fixed his green sprig in his cap. Letter from William McCleland to *The Irish-American,* January 10, 1863, Irish Brigade file, Fredericksburg and Spotsylvania National Military Park. Hereinafter cited as FSNMP. Lieutenant Colonel Mulholland of the 116th Pennsylvania wrote: "Wreaths were made and hung upon the tattered [U.S.] flags, and the national color of the Emerald Isle blended in fair harmony with the red, white, and blue of the Republic." Mulholland, *116th Pennsylvania*, p. 44. The ceremony with the green boxwood fired up the troops with unusual zeal and determination. Conyngham, *The Irish Brigade*, pp. 330-337, 341.

13. The Irish Brigade actually numbered about 1,200 men as the advance began. *OR* 21, p. 241.

14. Private William McCarter is incorrect regarding the deployment of the brigade. The 69th New York was placed at the head of the column so that it would form the right flank, followed by the 88th New York, 28th Massachusetts, 63rd New York, and 116th Pennsylvania. Ibid., pp. 241, 242.

15. Sergeant Marley was beheaded by the shell which wounded McCarter and killed three other men. Mulholland, *116th Pennsylvania*, p. 45.

16. Hancock's brigades charged in succession. Zook went first, followed by Meagher, and then Caldwell. Ibid., pp. 45, 46.

17. A fellow Irishman in the 8th Ohio, part of French's division, attempted to shelter himself by taking cover on the ground, from which point he observed the soldiers of the Irish Brigade as they charged the heights. "Every man has a sprig of green in his cap and a half-laughing, half-murderous look in his eye," he wrote. Captain Thomas F. Galwey, *The Valiant Hours* (Harrisburg, 1961), p. 62.

18. While the Irish Brigade took severe casualties from Confederate shells and canister, it was the heavy rifle fire from Thomas Cobb's Georgians that stalled the movement against Marye's Heights. "Round shot, grape and canister swept through the rank of the five regiments, but not for a moment did they halt until fire from the 'stone wall' became deadly—a steady, withering sheet of flame," remembered Maj. John Dwyer of the 63rd New York. "Address of John Dwyer," December 12, 1914, New York City, N.Y., Irish Brigade file, FSNMP. "None of our company fell until we were within 30 or 40 yards of the rifle pits, where we met dreadful showers of bullets from three lines of the enemy, besides their enfilading fire," wrote a New Yorker from the 88th regiment, Pvt. William McCleland. "Our men were mowed down like grass before the scythe of the reaper." Letter of William McCleland to *The Irish-American*, January 10, 1863, Irish Brigade file, FSNMP.

19. Many of Cobb's Georgians were Irish immigrants themselves. Lieutenant Colonel Mulholland alleged that these Southerners recognized the green flag of the 28th Massachusetts and the symbolic sprigs of green in their opponents' caps. "'Oh, God, what a pity! Here comes Meagher's fellows!' was the cry in the Confederate ranks," penned Mulholland. Nevertheless, Cobb's Georgians decimated the ranks of the Irish Brigade with accurate rifle fire. Mulholland, *116th Pennsylvania*, p. 57.

20. Like McCarter, Col. Robert Nugent, commanding the 69th New York, was overwhelmed by the casualties and brutal Rebel musketry. "The fire was terrific," he wrote, "no pen can describe the horrors of this battle. The casualties were enormous. It was a living hell from which escape seemed scarcely possible. I was myself carried off the field, having been shot through the right side." Robert Nugent, "The Sixty-ninth

Regiment at Fredericksburg," Third Annual Report of the Historian of the State of New York, 1897 (Albany, 1898), p. 42.

21. According to McCarter, "The sound, or song of the bullet as it is often called, in passing close to the head and ear, is exactly the same as that produced by a person pronouncing the word 'whist' very quickly in a sharp, slow, whispter." *My Life in the Army.*

22. Colonel Brynes of the 28th Massachusetts and Col. Patrick Kelly of the 88th New York met a fenceline not far below the stone wall and agreed to retreat, collecting what remained of the Irish Brigade. *OR* 21, p. 252. General Meagher met groups of survivors as they stumbled back down the slope, directing them toward a relatively safe location in town. By late afternoon, he had collected only 250 of the 1,200 men in the brigade. Ibid., p. 243.

23. Lieutenant Christian Foltz was the only officer in the 116th Pennsylvania to be killed outright at Marye's Heights. Lieutenant Robert Montgomery was mortally wounded, dying later that day, while Lt. Robert T. McGuire died of his wounds received at Fredericksburg during the spring of 1865. Mulholland, *116th Pennsylvania*, "Roll of Honor—The Dead of the 116th Pennsylvania."

24. Major General Oliver O. Howard's attack failed as miserably as the ones which had preceded it. See generally, Edward J. Stackpole, *The Fredericksburg Campaign: Drama on the Rappahannock* (Harrisburg, 1991), pp. 209-214.

25. Numerous Federal troops took shelter in and behind a brick farmhouse on the slope of Marye's Heights. The wounded in particular sought shelter there. Galwey, *The Valiant Hours*, pp. 60, 61.

26. McCarter, *My Life in the Army.*

27. *OR* 21, p. 128. The Irish Brigade lost 46 killed, 416 wounded, and 74 missing in action.

28. Conyngham, *The Irish Brigade*, pp. 351, 352.

Stonewall Jackson's Artillerists and the Defense of the Confederate Right

Gregory A. Mertz

D uring a war in which infantry was king and the number of minie balls finding their mark usually determined the outcome of battle, artillery played a secondary role. Although the Battle of Fredericksburg was no exception, the artillery posted on the Confederate right occupied key positions that proved quite significant as the battle unfolded. Nearly as important were the Federal reactions in consequence to Confederate artillery operations and the impact those judgments had on the contest.

From the fall of 1862 to the spring of 1863, the Confederates gradually incorporated significant changes in the organization of their artillery. As the most technical branch of the military, the artillery had become specialized to such a degree that an organization that assigned artillery batteries to infantry brigades was obsolete. A structure grouping the artillery together was needed, and a battalion system began to take shape shortly after the Battle of Sharpsburg (Antietam). Most artillerymen welcomed the changes—but not all, particularly at first. Captain William T. Poague of the Rockbridge Artillery wrote, "Our battery was loath to leave the old Stonewall Brigade of which it had been a part since the very beginning of the war."[1] Captain Carter M. Braxton, of the Fredericksburg Artillery, was pessimistic about the change. In a letter of October 11, 1862 he lamented that, "all the artillery of the Division has been thrown together permanently—much to my sorrow." His regrets may have been based more on the selection of Lt. Col. Reuben Lindsay Walker as the head of the artillery in Maj. Gen. A. P. Hill's Light Division than the change in organization. Braxton asserted that Walker was striving to administer some unspecified rules "in which he has & will fail."[2] The next battle for the Army of Northern Virginia artillerymen would be a good test to gauge whether or not the changes were a step in the right direction. That battle would be Fredericksburg.

As the Confederates studied Federal activities over the weeks prior to the Battle of Fredericksburg in order to determine when and where the anticipated offensive would be made, Confederate units were widely separated. Once the Federals crossed the Rappahannock River, the Confederates concentrated along a seven mile front. Lieutenant General James Longstreet's First Corps occupied more than four miles of lines on the Confederate left, with his left flank anchored on the Rappahannock River. The army's second corps, led by Lt. Gen. Thomas J. "Stonewall" Jackson, held a two mile front on the army's right flank. Major General James Ewell Brown (J.E.B) Stuart, with his division of cavalry, held about a mile of front on the extreme Confederate right, anchoring that flank of the army on Massaponax Creek. The disparity in the area defended by the two corps of nearly equal size is easily explained by considering the contrast in terrain. Most of Longstreet's line was on an impressive ridge, including Marye's Heights, while Jackson's divisions held a low ridge which would be much more difficult to defend than Longstreet's line. As a result, the strength of Jackson's position would be in the depth of reserves posted in rear of his front ranks. Jackson's front was entrusted to A. P. Hill's Division, while all three of the other divisions in the corps—under Maj. Gens. Daniel H. Hill, Jubal A. Early, and Brig. Gen. William B. Taliaferro—made up the reserve.

The strongest point of the position A. P. Hill selected was Prospect Hill, a modest rise and the first elevation north of the Massaponax Valley. The Richmond, Fredericksburg and Potomac Railroad ran across the front of Prospect Hill, about 200 yards away from its crest. The railroad curled around the southern part of the hill, intersecting with a road at a locale known as Hamilton's Crossing. The front of the hill, as well as the fields stretching toward the Federal position, were open. In a piece of low ground north of Prospect Hill, a tree line extended about 1/2 mile past the railroad. Hill's chief of artillery, Lt. Col. Reuben Lindsay Walker, had enough space to post fourteen guns on Prospect Hill. The six guns on the right of Walker's line were directed by Capt. William J. Pegram, of the Purcell Artillery. The eight guns on the left were led by Capt. David G. McIntosh, of the Pee Dee Artillery.[3]

Between the fourteen gun emplacements built to protect each of the gun crews was "a shallow trench," as David McIntosh described it. The trench afforded protection for two regiments of Col. John M. Brockenbrough's Brigade while providing support for the gunners, with the other half of the brigade lined up in rear of the artillery.[4] James J. Archer's Brigade formed to the left of Walker's artillery.

About 600 yards northwest of Archer's left was the right flank of James H. Lane's Brigade, positioned along the railroad bed. To the north of Lane's North Carolinians the Confederate artillery took advantage of another knoll offering a good field of fire to the front. Situated on the slope and the adjacent fields were the modest abodes for slaves who worked on Alfred Bernard's plantation; soldiers referred to the site as the Bernard Cabins. To the right of the field was a wood line.

Walker assigned Capt. Greenlee Davidson, of the Letcher Artillery, to head up the group of cannon on that portion of the field. Nine guns were initially posted at the Bernard Cabins but, later in the action, five additional pieces under Capt. Joseph Latimer, Jubal Early's chief of artillery, were used to either augment or replace some of Davidson's weapons.[5]

About 300 yards to the front of Davidson's artillery, the railroad bed sheltered pickets from the 16th North Carolina of William Dorsey Pender's Brigade. The Confederates established their skirmish line another 100 yards beyond Pender's pickets. The main infantry line and Davidson's support—the remainder of Pender's Brigade—were about 300 or 400 yards in rear of the cannon, inside the western border of the field.[6]

Davidson proclaimed his post "the weakest point on the line" and he may well have been correct.[7] The Bernard Cabins artillery line composed the left of Jackson's line, where it joined with Maj. Gen. John Bell Hood's Division on the right of Longstreet's Corps. While it is generally true that Longstreet's men had a defense in terrain, such was hardly the case on his extreme right. Hood's division held the Lansdowne Valley, a piece of ground on the Confederate right-center lower in elevation than the terrain occupied by any other infantry division of the Army of Northern Virginia.

Despite the lack of altitude, Hood's line was not without its attributes. His front was in the shape of a reentrant—a U-shaped line formed exactly the opposite from a salient. Across the mouth of the reentrant were two brigades, ostensibly prolonging Jackson's line northward, but these two units were hardly expected to attempt any real defense in the poor position that they held. Once these two advanced brigades fell back to Hood's main line, any federal force advancing against Hood's center would be subjected to simultaneous enfilading fire from Hood's right and left. As long as Hood's flanks were protected, he would likely have little problem defending his line. Davidson's gunners, therefore, held a key position: they were entrusted with holding the seam between Hood's forward right flank *and* Jackson's reserve-packed left flank. It would prove a difficult task.

Although Davidson felt that his guns held the weakest spot of the Confederate line, a good argument could be made for one other point as well. Colonel Stapleton Crutchfield, chief of artillery for Jackson's Corps, believed that "the center of the line was our weakest part." The middle of Jackson's line was a low, forested marshland. This area contained the woods to the left of the Prospect Hill guns and the right of the Bernard Cabins' artillery. The woods represented a 600-yard gap in the Confederate infantry line between the brigades of Archer and Lane. The only soldiers posted in the interval were pickets along the railroad bed. Crutchfield based his declaration of the center being the "weakest part" because Walker's fourteen guns on Prospect Hill "could not oblique their fire to the left sufficiently" to keep Federal infantry from reaching the woods. Likewise, Davidson's guns on the other side of the woods could not prevent the enemy infantrymen from reaching the swampy forest either. Crutchfield estimated a stretch between 800 yards and 1,000 yards existed in the Confederate line which was "undefended by a direct artillery fire to the front."[8]

In an attempt to remedy this problem, Crutchfield inspected Jackson's center, seeking a place from which howitzers might be able to blast canister at any force seizing the gap. To his dismay, however, he found the "undergrowth so think as to require more time to clear it away than we had before the action began." Instead, Crutchfield had to settle for additional artillery positions beyond the main line of defense to deter the Federals from entering the wood. Crutchfield selected a position east of the railroad and about 400 yards to the right-front of Davidson for this purpose.[9] Captain John B. Brockenbrough, acting chief of artillery for Taliaferro's Division, was in charge of this collection of twelve guns. Crutchfield indicated that the guns on the left of Jackson's line "more directly controlled" the woods than Walker's Prospect Hill guns, "but only by a quite oblique fire to the right. . ."[10]

Another group of artillery was also placed in advance of the main line, positioned to pound any Federals heading toward the gap from the south side of the woods. In the open plains of the Massaponax Valley, Maj. John Pelham, chief of artillery for the cavalry division, assembled a sizeable artillery force. This force consisted of some—if not all—of the five batteries making up the Stuart Horse Artillery.[11] Before the action got underway, Pelham sought out other guns to supplement his own command. Colonel J. Thompson Brown, commanding a battalion of the artillery reserve, responded by sending eight guns to Pelham's aid at about noon, and Jubal Early's Division loaned seven of their own cannon to the horse artillery.[12] Jackson indicated in his after-action report of the battle that this collection of artillery assembled from various com-

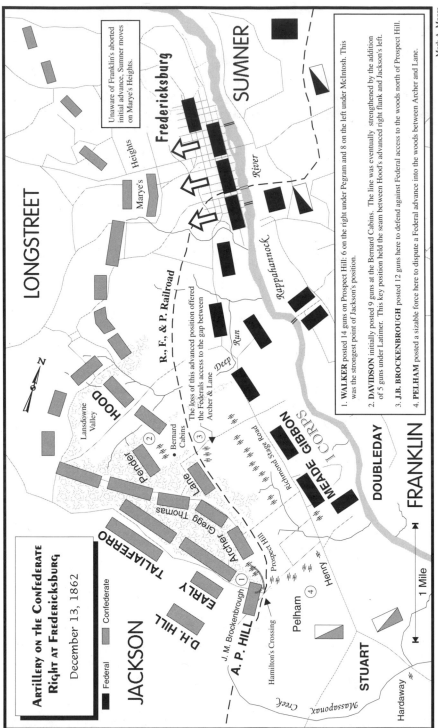

ARTILLERY ON THE CONFEDERATE
Right at Fredericksburg
December 13, 1862

Federal
Confederate

Unaware of Franklin's aborted
initial advance, Sumner moves
on Marye's Heights.

Mark A. Moore

1. **WALKER** posted 14 guns on Prospect Hill: 6 on the right under Pegram and 8 on the left under McIntosh. This
was the strongest point of Jackson's position.

2. **DAVIDSON** initially posted 9 guns at the Bernard Cabins. The line was eventually strengthened by the addition
of 5 guns under Latimer. This key position held the seam between Hood's advanced right flank and Jackson's left.

3. **J.B. BROCKENBROUGH** posted 12 guns here to defend against Federal access to the woods north of Prospect Hill.

4. **PELHAM** posted a sizable force here to dispute a Federal advance into the woods between Archer and Lane.

The loss of this advanced position offered
the Federals access to the gap between
Archer & Lane.

mands was "thrown into position so as to cross their fire with the guns of Lieutenant-Colonel Walker, and designed to check the advance of the enemy in that direction."[13]

Although a cavalry commander, J. E. B. Stuart possessed a good eye for artillery and played an active role in the placement of the guns. Staff officer R. Channing Price wrote that Stuart's task was "to bring and bear a large number of guns and break the left flank of the enemy." Stuart accordingly selected and stayed at a location where he had a good view of the enemy, so he could observe their movement and "know when to begin his work," as Price later phrased it.[14]

William S. White, in the 3rd Richmond Howitzers of Brown's Battalion, accompanied two Parrott rifles detached to serve with Pelham. Despite noting the low elevation and the vulnerability of being posted in open ground, White noticed their position had the positive aspect of limiting the field available to the Federals for maneuver and "necessarily kept the enemy confined in a much smaller space than his great numbers warranted."[15]

South of Massaponax Creek was one more cannon worth noting. Captain Robert A. Hardaway's (Alabama) Battery, assigned to D. H. Hill's Division, boasted a British-made, breech-loading Whitworth rifle with a three-mile effective range. This piece dropped trail to the far right, and was naturally placed where any other cannon in the army would have been virtually worthless.[16]

With both Brockenbrough and Pelham in forward positions on either side of the forested marsh and the corresponding gap in the Confederate infantry line, the Southern gunners had done their best to cover the vulnerable center of Jackson's line. Even though the front line consisted of only one infantry division, the supporting artillery contained guns from each of the four divisions of Jackson's Corps, from Stuart's Horse Artillery, and Brig. Gen. William Nelson Pendleton's artillery reserve.

The battalion system was designed to allow for the placement of artillery where it was needed the most and could render the best service—regardless of the assignment given to the infantry division to which the batteries were attached. The placement of the artillery at Fredericksburg was the first combat-tested operation of the battalion system, and it appeared to be achieving its goal.

With the batteries set in positions of their choosing, the gunners peered into a fog. Despite the poor visibly, as the fog veiled the Federal activities from the Southern gunners, "we had abundant evidences" wrote Greenlee Davidson at the Bernard Cabins, "that the enemy was busily at work." Davidson heard, "the rattling of the artillery wheels. . .commands given to the infantry. . .the brass band. . .and the music," recognizing these as the sounds of Federal battle preparations.[17]

Other aspects of the weather would impact the battle in other ways. Private Carter Nelson Berkley Minor, a member of the Rockbridge Artillery in Pelham's group, noted the unusually mild weather of December 12, calling it an "Indian Summer." J. W. F. Hatton, in Dement's Maryland Battery, writing of December 13 noted, "the day was a fine one for the season of the year—and suited for the event to occur."[18]

But certain aspects of the warm weather were not particularly well-suited for the artillery. Prior to the battle, the weather had been quite cold, with prolonged freezing temperatures that froze the ground solid. The warmer temperatures just before and during the battle thawed the earth, and the surface turned to mud.[19] Cannon wheels needed to turn freely and trails needed to slide along the ground each time a fired artillery piece recoiled. The resistance presented by the sticky muck of thawing soil would place a great deal of stress on gun carriages.

As the artillerymen waited for the battle to begin, many of them were not stationed at their actual battle positions. All along the line, gunners were given similar instructions to conceal themselves and their guns from enemy view. Thus, even when the fog finally lifted, and the Federals could see across the fields as well as the human eye could discern, they could not tell the exact location of the Confederate position and would be forced to try to stir the rebels up from their cover.

The Federals amassing before the Confederate right numbered some 65,000 soldiers, about half of Maj. Gen. Ambrose E. Burnside's Army of the Potomac. The troops opposite Jackson were under the immediate command of Maj. Gen. William B. Franklin. The responsibility for the primary Federal attack rested on Franklin's shoulders—although he apparently did not appreciate this. Unfortunately for the Federals, the plan which Burnside verbally discussed with Franklin and his subordinates the evening prior to the contest, and the written orders Franklin received on the morning of the battle, did not match. Burnside intended for Franklin to make a substantial attack and take Prospect Hill. Once Franklin's attack was underway, another force under Maj. Gen. Edwin Vose Sumner was to move out from the streets of Fredericksburg, about four miles north of Prospect Hill, and launch an attack against Marye's Heights. The purpose of advancing on Marye's Heights would be to prevent the Confederates from stripping their left for reinforcements to be sent against Franklin. Everything hinged upon Franklin. On the morning of December 13, 1862, Franklin's forces lined up parallel to the Richmond Stage Road, preparing for an attack toward "Stonewall" Jackson's line.

The first aggressive action taken by either side on what would prove to be a day of intense bloodshed was initiated by a lone gun manned by Confederate horse artillerymen from Capt. Mathis Winston Henry's Battery. As the Federals formed in the fog for their attack, Confederates appreciated that a force making very little noise—thus necessarily small—could gain the Federal left flank. George W. Shreve, one of the gunners accompanying the solitary cannon, indicated that he and his comrades "crept slowly from Hamilton's Crossing down into the plain" and silently formed behind a cedar hedge.[19] The gunners could tell from a reconnaissance made with their ears that enemy voices came from a distance of a few hundred yards away. Not until they were able to see well enough to locate the enemy through the fog would they be able to take advantage of their position. For the moment they had to be content to wait a while longer, poised in readiness for the opportunity to begin the fray. As the fog gradually dissipated, watchful eyes through the gaps in the hedge identified the Federal position before them. "Pelham was exactly on their left flank with his gun," wrote Lt. Richard Channing Price of Stuart's staff, "with no support whatever."[20] The Rebel gunners were perfectly situated to fire down the line of the still forming Federal force.

Such a tremendous opportunity was likewise accompanied with great risk. Being so close to such a large enemy force, with few supports close at hand, the gunners were acutely aware of their perilous situation. Despite "fearing annihilation at their [Federal] hands," Shreve reported, "we commenced firing." Rather than "rushing for us, and overwhelming us with their numbers,"—a likely Federal response Shreve was bracing for—he was relieved to discover that "the unexpected presence of our guns so close to them, seemed to paralyse them."[21]

Of the Federal forces subjected to this surprise cannon fire down their flank, the artillery branch was the quickest to make adjustments. Shreve recalled that the first retaliatory shot was received while his detachment was "in the act of loading the second charge." The number one member of the gun crew, responsible for handling the ramrod and sponge staff, was a gunner named "Hammond." While swabbing the barrel after the first shot was fired, "a shell from the enemy's gun, cut him down, and he had time only to say 'tell mother I die bravely.'"[22]

John Esten Cooke, of Stuart's staff, thought about twelve Yankee pieces fired back at Pelham's lone gun. Price, however, estimated the Federal artillery

Captain Greenlee Davidson, of the Letcher Artillery, headed up a group of cannon posted around the Bernard Cabins. Davidson proclaimed his position "the weakest point on the line," because the fourteen guns on Prospect Hill "could not oblique their fire to the left sufficiently" to keep Federal infantry from reaching the woods.the housed the Confederate line. *Captain Greenlee Davidson, C.S.A.*

Maj. Gen. A. P. Hill's chief of artillery, **Lt. Col. Reuben Lindsey Walker**, posted fourteen guns on Prospect Hill. In order to conceal their positions, the gunners had strict orders not to permit themselves to be drawn into an artillery duel. When Walker's artillery cluster was subjected to enemy artillery fire, they were to ignore it and withhold their return fire for enemy infantry. *Image of War*

Maj. John Pelham, the chief of artillery of the Stuart Horse Artillery, positioned a single artillery piece on the far left of the Federal army. "Pelham was exactly on their left flank with his gun," wrote Lt. R. C. Price of Stuart's staff, "with no support whatever." Pelham was perfectly situated to fire down the line of the still forming Federal force. *Miller's Photographic History*

Capt. William T. Poague, of the Rockbridge Artillery. Two of the artillery pieces sent to Prospect Hill werePoague's large 20-pounder Parrott rifles, and Stonewall Jackson gave him special instructions to fire upon an enemy battery. His shots seemingly stirred up a hornet's nest, attracting a fearsome return fire during what had been a relatively quiet period on Prospect Hill. *Long Arm of Lee*

The six guns on the right of Walker's line were directed by **Capt. William J. Pegram**, of the Purcell Artillery. While Pegram and Lt. James Ellett were talking, a shell exploded sbove them. Pegram, always in the hottest spot on any field, continued to lead a charmed life and was unharmed. Ellett, however, was struck by a hot fragment of iron and instantly killed. *Long Arm of Lee*

The eight guns on the left of Walkers line were led by **Capt. David G. McIntosh**, of the Pee Dee Artillery. When the Federal guns opened up on the Confederates, McIntosh flirted with danger. He leaned on a sapling, and with arms crossed, looked in the direction of the enemy while the soil about him was being cultivated by "missles [sic] of death." *Long Arm of Lee*

response consisted of some fifteen or twenty cannon. Although Captain Henry's gunners directed their fire primarily toward Federal infantry, one of the shots found a Yankee caisson, causing it to go up in smoke.[23]

After harassing the Federal flank for about twenty minutes, the gun crew was "commanded to cease, and to lie flat on the ground," recalled Shreve. While in this prone position, shot and shell fell all around the gunners—a solid shot decapitating one of them. The cedar hedge concealed the gunners so that most Federal shots landed long.[24]

At some point during the unequal contest the cavalry chief decided the solitary gun crew needed assistance. "I was sent by Stuart for an additional gun," wrote Cooke, "which was posted nearer the crossing and opened fire." The weapon Cooke sent to Henry's aid was a British manufactured Blakely rifle. After firing one shot, the Blakely's gunners were targeted by Federal artillerymen and the "first shell thrown by them struck the gun," lamented Cooke, "and dismounted it, killing two of the men." Except for the shot fired by the Blakely and a little cavalry detail "to guard Pelham's gun from a rush of sharpshooters," Captain Henry's gun crew fought on their own.[25]

After spending a short time on the ground, Henry's Napoleon gun crew once again sprung to their feet to resume menacing the Federals. Then, after a short time, they were sent to the rear. Apparently the gunners had authority to withdraw—perhaps even orders requiring withdrawal—before the gunners gave up their stance on the Federal flank. Heros von Borcke, of Stuart's staff, indicated that he relayed a message from Stuart "to tell Pelham to retire if he thought the proper moment had arrived." The head of Stuart's Horse Artillery responded, "Tell the General I can hold my ground." According to von Borcke, "three times the summons to retire was renewed," but only after firing the final round left in their limber chest did the gunners forfeit their advanced position.[26]

While most of the credit for the daring displayed that morning has been credited to Pelham, John Cheves Haskell indicated that he spoke with Pelham "several times" about the achievement and vouched that the leader of mounted artillerymen "freely gave credit to Henry." While von Borcke later claimed that Pelham refused to obey orders to withdraw, Pelham in turn told Haskell that it was Henry who disputed Pelham's order to withdraw. Pelham apparently told Haskell how Henry rationalized that he had only lost two men "and thought he better stay." (The battery would officially suffer six men wounded through the duration of the battle.) Certainly there is enough praise to go around involving this feat for Captain Henry to be credited with aggressiveness and daring, and Pelham for good command judgment and prudence.[27]

Price maintained that the reason Pelham was pulled back was so the Federals "might come up closer to our line." General Robert E. Lee apparently desired to allow the Federals to get within range of additional Confederate artillery before *any* shots were fired. According to Price, Lee "said that the young Major-General (alluding to Stuart) had opened on them too soon."[28]

While the commanding general was somewhat critical of Stuart, he was impressed with Pelham. "General Lee expressed his warm admiration for Major Pelham's distinguished gallantry," wrote Channing Price. On the day of the battle, Lee wrote to Secretary of War James A. Seddon of Pelham's accomplishments, referring to him as "the gallant Pelham." Lee reported that "he sustained their heavy fire with the unflinching courage that ever distinguished him." The *London Times* printed an account of the battle, reporting Lee to have said of Pelham, "It is inspiriting to see such glorious courage in one so young."[29]

Jackson's report described Pelham's action as "a brisk and animated contest" and estimated the duration to be "about an hour." The same *London Times* article mentioned above suggests that Jackson was engaged in some wishful thinking, quoting him as saying, "With a Pelham upon either flank I could vanquish the world." Jackson apparently decided he could settle for just one Pelham as Cooke heard "Stonewall" tell Stuart, "If you have another Pelham I wish you would give him to me."[30]

The most substantial consequence of this single gun's action does not lie in the tactical advantage this small unit gained over a much larger force, or the daring of the Confederate commanders involved. Rather, the most important result lies in the Federal reaction. Fearing the possibility of such a threat reoccurring from that sector, the Federals made preparations to deal with that contingency. While it was indeed wise and prudent to do so, the manner in which the Federals responded is most perplexing.

The troops Franklin selected to assault the Confederate position—and the force Pelham's gun fired upon—were from Maj. Gen. John F. Reynolds' First Corps. This corps contained three divisions, with Brig. Gen. John Gibbon's on the right, Maj. Gen. George G. Meade's in the center, and Brig. Gen. Abner Doubleday's on the left. Doubleday was not only to protect the left flank of the corps, but the left flank of the entire army. With the appearance of Pelham's gun, Doubleday concluded that he could not do both—in which he was quite correct. Instead of assigning another body of troops the task of making sure the site of Pelham's gun remained secure, Doubleday's division was withdrawn from the assaulting force. Meade was expected to fare for his left flank himself. The primary attack of the Army of the Potomac, as envisioned by Burnside, would eventually be made with only two divisions rather than the three divisions which were intended to be used before Pelham's gun appeared near the Richmond Stage Road. The most significant consequence of Captain Henry's blazing gun was the Federal reaction—the decision to weaken the upcoming attack by one-third of its strength before the battle had hardly begun. Thus, instead of 16,000 Federals moving toward A. P. Hill and the various Confederate artillery groups, only 10,000 would be attempting the same feat.[31]

In the lull following the opening of the battle, the Federals made their adjustments to protect their left flank, redress the lines disrupted by Pelham's gun, and bring forward additional troops. With the fog dissipated, some Confederates nervously watched the Federal preparations. "I felt uneasy" by the sight of the Federals forming in plain view, wrote an artilleryman in McIntosh's Pee Dee artillery on Prospect Hill, "until I saw Gen. Lee, and right behind him the 'Old Stonewall,' riding up and down our lines, looking at the foe as cooly [sic] and calmly as if they were only going to have a general muster."[32]

The Federals finally initiated the first step of their plan by opening with an artillery barrage directed toward Jackson's men. The goal of the bombardment was to soften the Confederate line in preparation for the two-division infantry assault. The problem was that the Federal artillerymen did not know precisely where their proper targets were to be found, and the Confederates were not going provide any assistance.

In addition to taking careful steps to conceal their positions, Confederate gunners had strict orders concerning when and how to respond. Walker's artillerists were instructed not to permit themselves to be drawn into an artillery duel. When Walker's artillery cluster at Prospect Hill were subjected to enemy artillery fire, they were to ignore it and withhold their return fire for enemy "infantry when it should come into effective range." True to their orders, not a gun replied on the Confederate line. "It was hard to take," admitted a South Carolina artilleryman under McIntosh, "but we had strict orders not to fire."[33]

When the shelling began, at about 9:30 a.m., artillerist Willie Pegram was notifying Lt. James Ellett where to place his two guns of the Crenshaw Artillery. Earlier in the day, when Ellett's guns were detached from the others in the battery, he "shook hands with and bade those he left behind good bye, as if he felt that he would never see them again." While Pegram and Ellett were talking, a shell exploded over their heads. The aggressive Pegram, who always seemed to be in the hottest artillery spot on any battlefield, continued to lead a charmed life and was unharmed. Ellett, however, was not so fortunate, and a hot fragment of iron struck and instantly killed him. His brother, Sgt. Robert Ellett, was near at hand when the fatality occurred, and he rode off to tell the sad news to another brother, Thomas, as well as the men in the other section of the battery.[34]

Despite shelling the entire general area in their front, most of the Federal shells did little damage since the Federals could determine nothing to indicate when their rounds were inflicting injury. Sensing little harm from the Federal shelling, some Confederates flirted with danger. Captain McIntosh selected a sapling to lean upon, and with arms crossed looked in the direction of the enemy while the soil about him was being cultivated by "missles [sic] of death." John Payne, a veteran of every battle the Crenshaw Artillery had witnessed, took a rather nonchalant attitude toward the bombardment and calmly stood in contrast to the rest of his prone battery mates. When reproached by an officer, Payne responded, "If I was born to die in battle. . .I'll be killed just as quick laying down as standing up." The fatalist gunner was killed instantly that day—he and Ellett being the only deaths in the Crenshaw Artillery during the battle.[35]

One section of the Rockbridge Artillery held a position near Massaponax Creek. They were close enough to the waterway for artilleryman Minor to note that Federal shots fired long of their mark would "drop with a great splash" into the waters.[36] After a tremendous exhibition, the bombardment stopped with the Federals not knowing that their barrage had caused great splashes, torn off many tree limbs, burned a lot of powder, and fatigued several hundred Federal gunners—but accomplished little else. Optimistically hoping that the Confederate line had suffered significant damage, the two divisions of Meade and Gibbon were sent forward.

In accordance with their instructions, Confederate artillerymen took their posts as the Federal infantry moved toward them, then patiently waited for the blue lines to reach a point within deadly range of their cannon. Confederate guns were already trained at predetermined points within 800 yards of the guns, and the men had cut fuses to match the carefully estimated distance. For McIntosh's cannoneers on Prospect Hill, the landmark was "a tree standing out by itself just beyond the line of the railroad." Meade and Gibbon's men came on impressively, reached the tree McIntosh had been eyeing, and the battle escalated to a new level.[37]

Jackson boasted that the batteries on Prospect Hill poured "such a storm of shot and shell into [the Federal] ranks as to cause him first to halt, then to waver, and at last seek shelter by flight." The Confederate artillery brought the divisions under Meade and Gibbon to a halt. It became quickly obvious to the Federals that their bombardment had been ineffective, but at least they had finally learned where the Confederates were located. With this information in hand, the Federals decided to start their assault anew. Meade and Gibbon were pulled out of range of the punishing Confederate guns and regrouped. The first round was over; superbly placed Confederate artillery stopped 10,000 Federals before most of the Confederate infantry had a opportunity to fire a shot. Federal gunners were given another chance to strike the Confederate positions—now that they saw where their proper targets were.[38]

Just as it was with the first Confederate artillery action of the day, however, the Army of Northern Virginia benefited from yet another critical Federal decision made in consequence of the disruption of the Federal infantry assault. Burnside planned to initiate Edwin Sumner's attacks against Marye's Heights *after* Franklin's offensive had developed. Civil War era communications made it exceedingly difficult to coordinate such movements, however, and Burnside's calculation of when Franklin's attack became general would be imperfect at best. Aware that Franklin's two divisions had advanced, and hearing the heavy fire of Confederate artillery, Burnside presumed that Meade and Gibbon had closed with the enemy and the time was right to order the diversion against Marye's Heights. Unaware that the troops that had stepped off toward Jackson's line had postponed their further advance to give the Federal artillerymen one more crack at the Confederates confronting them, Sumner's men were sent forward against Longstreet's nearly impregnable position. The premature advance of Sumner's men meant that they had even less chance of success than they might otherwise have had, and that the disastrous back-to-back assaults that would continue all day long until darkness brought a close to the battle secured an earlier start than intended, and a longer casualty list probably resulted.[39]

While the first of Sumner's attacks against the strongest section of the Confederate line were being broken to pieces, the Federal cannoneers resumed their fire, honing in on the artillery groupings of Pelham, Walker, Davidson and Brockenbrough. The Southern gunners began to suffer casualties as a result. Brockenbrough's guns were particularly vulnerable to Federal artillery fire. Being advanced nearly to the skirmish line, his pieces were closer to the enemy than the other groupings, and since Brockenbrough's men were positioned to direct an oblique line of fire to their right, their left flank was partially exposed. Captain John C. Carpenter's Battery held the unprotected left end of the line, and its commander, Lt. George McKendree, observed Federal artillery "attempting to enfilade our position." McKendree requested two batteries to his left-rear—Davidson's artillery group—"to begin firing at once, and, if possible, dislodge the [Federal] pieces." McKendree complained that their response was "a very slow fire," which did not succeed in "driving the enemy from his position" nor divert any fire away from McKendree by "attracting the firing in that direction." Because of the destructive fire, Carpenter's Battery soon had only enough men to fire three of its four guns, and was eventually compelled to withdraw "another piece, and placed all the available men I then had to the two remaining guns."[40]

In addition to the cannon firing on the left flank of Brockenbrough's twelve pieces, sharpshooters persistently executed their talents on the gunners. The sharpshooters were "annoying us greatly" reported Crutchfield, and were "working around the right of Captain Brockenbrough's position." Despite the effectiveness of canister fire on the marksmen, they were "protected by the accidents of the ground and so feebly opposed by our own sharpshooters," complained Crutchfield, "that they could not be entirely dislodged, and caused heavy loss in our batteries, both among men and horses."[41]

Among the casualties from the artillery fire on their left and sharpshooter fire on their right was Brockenbrough himself, who was wounded. Captain G. W. Wooding of the Danville Artillery, was "badly shot while acting as gunner to one of his pieces," and a gun in the battery was disabled with a broken axle from the recoil action—probably related to the thick mud on the field. Two lieutenants were wounded and another lieutenant was killed among Brockenbrough's officer corps.[42]

If McKendree felt the fire from Davidson's guns appeared "very slow," there may have been a logical reason for their dilatory employment. In Charles J. Raine's Battery at the Bernard Cabins, the shells taken from the limbers were so defective that Davidson replaced Raines' guns with others that possessed more effective ammunition. Crutchfield thought that none of the shells fired by Raine's battery exploded, and felt that defective fuses were the culprits.[43]

Coming to Davidson's aid and taking Raine's place as well as increasing the size of the force were five pieces under the direction of Early's artillery chief, the youthful Joseph W. Latimer. "The position on which these guns were posted was not a very advantageous one," demurred Latimer, "but the best that could be selected." Davidson observed the conduct and service of the mounted Latimer, who "looked as unconcerned as if he had been at a holiday frolic," even though enemy projectiles were passing by him.[44]

Latimer's gunners were engaged in some of the hottest action of the day, and his Chesapeake Artillery endured the loss of one gun disabled during the action. One of the artillerymen in that battery that provided the ammunition for his piece was cut in two by a projectile and "burned to a crisp." The soldier's uniform was stripped from him in the concussion "and blown into the top of a tall pine," wrote Davidson.[45]

Federal shot struck a limber chest of the Chesapeake gunners, causing a particularly dangerous situation. Not only did the terrible explosion spray metal fragments about the batteries, but the ensuing panic caused the six horses making up the team to wildly gallop about the knoll, dragging the damaged limber behind. Men from two of the gun crews were grazed by the tumbling limber, while ammunition was scattered about the position—some fifteen or twenty of which were ignited by the numerous sparks permeating the air from some fifteen cannon belching fire.[46]

In addition to the counter-artillery fire, Federal sharpshooters were also inflicting casualties on Latimer's gunners. While Crutchfield was critical of much of the infantry support—or lack thereof—that his batteries received, he credited Brig. Gen. Evander M. Law's Brigade of John Hood's Division with driving back the Federal sharpshooters harassing Latimer.[47]

Elsewhere on the Davidson-Latimer line of artillery, some artillerists handled the stress of battle with substantial composure. With each tug of the lanyard in one gun crew of the Letcher Artillery, Martin DeLaney appealed, "Lord be marsiful [sic] to their poor souls." Damage to men and material were high at the Bernard Cabins: Caskie's battery lost a gun from a broken axle—again a possible consequence of firing the weapon in thick mud.[48]

The Federals likewise hit their targets on Prospect Hill. "A Minie ball went through the ramrod, and it or a splinter struck me on the head," wrote a cannoneer in the Pee Dee Artillery identified only as "Ben." "I was by the gun looking at the Yankees when a great piece of shell, big as my two fists, came along and knocked a spoke out of the wheel," Ben wrote, "and it or a piece of the spoke, or something else, hit me square in the breast."[49] Alongside his battery of South Carolinians, Ben noted that the men of the Purcell Artillery "had left their guns." The Carolinian saw that the belligerent battery commander defied the example set by his own gunners. "Captain Pegram wrapped his battle flag around him," observed the cannoneer, "walking up and down among his deserted guns."[50]

The artillerymen on the Confederate right were enduring an exhausting day. Private Robert Fraser served in the section of the Rockbridge Artillery sent to Pelham at about noon. Except for moments when they necessarily halted fire "to let the guns cool," Fraser indicated there was only one period when they were not sending discharges toward Burnside's army—that was to maneuver their guns to "a more effective position." The steady firing required the caissons to be sent rearward in search of more ammunition from the ordnance trains.[51]

Another member of the Rockbridge Artillery, Pvt. Thomas M. Wade, observed Pelham riding amongst the guns, seemingly enjoying himself, "like a boy playing ball." Wade heard Pelham tell section commander Lt. Archibald Graham, "Your men stand killing better than any I know."[52]

Vivian Fleming of the 2nd Richmond Howitzers was also serving in the Massaponax Valley. He recalled that "a number of our guns were knocked from the trunions by their shell." The early workings of the battalion system seemed to be functioning as planned, however, for replacement pieces were brought forward and "the fight kept on," Fleming professed.[53]

Once the Federal commanders believed this second attempt by their artillery to soften the Confederate line had lasted of sufficient duration, the Union infantrymen were again sent forward to drive the Confederates from Prospect Hill and vicinity. The most vulnerable Confederate artillery position was Brockenbrough's; his men could not hope to hold their advanced position and the intrepid gunners withdrew. Brockenbrough called forward the infantry supports, which took a position "some 20 yards to our front, and held the enemy in check until we could limber up our two remaining guns." The gunners withdrew to a position to the left-rear of Davidson.[54]

Between the addition of Latimer's guns to the Bernard Cabins position and the detachments sent to bolster the guns in the Massaponax Valley, the Confederates had just about as many guns in line after the artillery duel as before. While the replacement cannon satisfactorily filled the role of the guns which had been disabled, the pieces sent to the rear with defective ammunition, and the crews which had suffered heavy losses, they could not make up for the loss of Brockenbrough's advantageous position. Once that battery site was abandoned, the route through the marshy woods and into the gap in the Confederate line was wide open to the advancing Federals.

The Federal infantry force—weakened by the initial Confederate artillery response and advancing again without any additional reinforcements to speak of—rolled forward with impetus. This time the Confederate artillery could not stop the entire line in their tracks as it had done before. Although the Unionists marching directly upon Prospect Hill were stopped by the combined artillery and musketry fire delved out from that sector, a portion of George Meade's command made it into the woods—and into the gap. To the south of the gap, Meade turned on Archer's infantry and Walker's artillery, but because of the depth in Jackson's lines, reinforcements were able to arrest the Federal progress

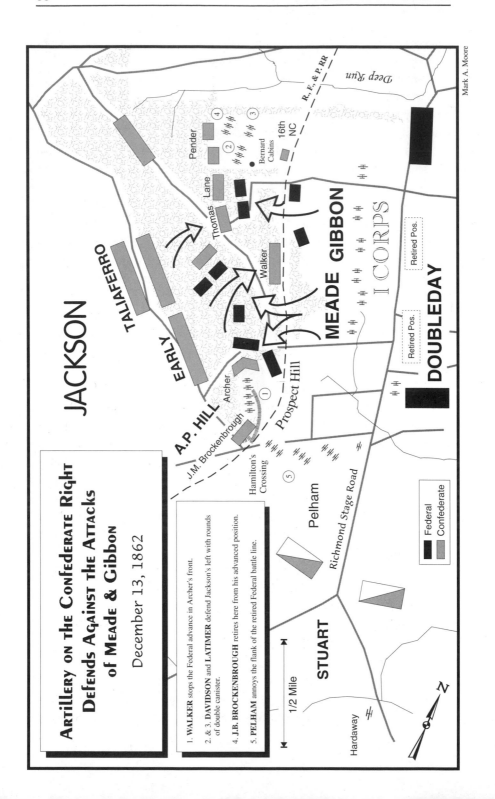

Artillery on the Confederate Right
Defends Against the Attacks
of Meade & Gibbon
December 13, 1862

1. **WALKER** stops the Federal advance in Archer's front.

2. & 3. **DAVIDSON** and **LATIMER** defend Jackson's left with rounds of double canister.

4. **J.B. BROCKENBROUGH** retires here from his advanced position.

5. **PELHAM** annoys the flank of the retired Federal battle line.

Federal
Confederate

1/2 Mile

N

Mark A. Moore

with some difficulty. Confederate regiments closest to the gap suffered heavy losses, had a battleflag captured, and sustained all of the typical indications of a tough fight, but the Prospect Hill cannon were apparently not in serious danger of falling into Federal hands. The Federals who turned Archer's flank were not properly supported by other units participating in the attack. While those Pennsylvanians who struck Archer's flank attempted to exploit their advantage, other comrades, expected to simultaneously pressure Archer's front, were stopped cold by Walker's flaming guns. The Prospect Hill section of the battle-field offered no hope for Federal success. The situation on the other side of the gap, however, was different.

While the portion of Meade's command that struck Lane's flank north of the gap was fighting to exploit its advantage, an entire division under John Gibbon was applying pressure against Lane's front. Lane's North Carolinians suffered the highest casualties of any Confederate brigade in the Battle of Fredericksburg and were driven from their position on the railroad. The Federals had done more than simply take the 600-yard gap; they had widened it by the margin of a brigade and were set to pitch into Davidson's Battery and Pender's supporting brigade. If successful in achieving their next objective, the Federals would be on Hood's susceptible right flank.

Davidson rightly grew concerned over the ability of the Pender's skirmish line to hold it's post. George H. Mills, of Pender's 16th North Carolina, recognized that the artillerymen at the Bernard Cabins were suffering from the effect of sharpshooters as well as the "perfect" aim of Federal artillerymen. "A brave officer of the battery," as Mills described Davidson, requested the commander of the 16th, Col. John S. McElroy, to "drive off the skirmishers and they would take care of the main body."[55]

William Dorsey Pender, who was with Davidson at the time, mounted his horse and rode to rally his skirmishers fighting on the right of the guns. The North Carolinian, however, was soon shot, and the partially rallied skirmishers broke for the rear. The withdrawal of Pender's men meant that Davidson "was left out in the open field to contend unaided against the advancing column. . . within a stone's throw of my guns."[56]

The situation called for double canister and Davidson's gunners "let them have it low." Three rounds from the line of guns at the Bernard Cabins cut down the lead troops before sending the remainder "to their heels," wrote Davidson, "and you never saw such a stampede in your life."[57]

After taking care of the Federals advancing straight on his guns, Davidson noticed other Yankees moving through the woods on his right. Davidson wrote,

"I expect[ed] to every moment see them dash out of the timber." The captain assessed that his batteries were "now in a critical position." Despite the perilous situation, Davidson reported that retreat was not one of his options; Jackson's orders were to "hold the position if it cost every man and gun."[58]

To his great relief, however, Davidson soon heard sounds indicating that desperately needed assistance had arrived, as "tremendous volleys of musketry rolling up from the woods to our right" were audible. The explosion of small arms fire came from the men of Brig. Gen. Edward L. Thomas' Georgia brigade, which was moving up from its reserve position.[59]

While Thomas and numerous other brigades from Jackson's multiple lines of reserves plugged the gap, the Federals made another dash for the Bernard Cabins artillery. But just as before, double canister rounds soon brought an end to the threat. Davidson concluded that the short range ammunition fired "from a Napoleon gun is a terrible engine of destruction."[60]

Davidson's defense of the Bernard Cabins and the counterattacks by the infantry reserves secured the Confederate position. The artillerymen under Brockenbrough, Davidson and Walker had had a hard day and their action was over, but Pelham still had designs on punishing the Federals even more.

After the Federals were repulsed, Pelham's group moved forward to try to constantly place their guns where they could continue an enfilading fire. When the Federals had withdrawn to the vicinity of where they had staged the attack, Pelham attempted to repeat his feat of earlier in the day. One gun from the 2nd Richmond Howitzers and another from the Rockbridge Artillery were sent forward. This time, however, they did not enjoy the cover of fog, nor were these gunners instructed to select a position screened by the cedar hedge. Instead, they were placed in a dangerously exposed position. "The neighborhood of these 2 Guns," declared Channing Price, "was I think the hottest place from Artillery fire that I have ever been in."[61]

The Richmonders were told to tear down a section of "wattling" fence and shovel spades of dirt into a ditch lining the Hamilton's Crossing Road in order to create an access into the open field. This placed the guns in front of the cedar hedge Henry's gunners had effectively utilized during their earlier action. Sergeant Reuben B. Pleasants of the 2nd Richmond Howitzers was instructed by cavalry Col. Thomas L. Rosser to select a position and "see what I had to do." A short reconnaissance revealed to Pleasants that his gun crew was "on the extreme left flank of the Army of the Potomac." Rosser instructed Pleasants to hold the position "as long as you can."[62]

Pleasants' detachment was "met by a salute from the enemy's guns" as soon as they rode into the field, but the crew and teams of horses rode on, up to within about five hundred yards of the Federals before they dropped trail. "There we were," Pleasants later mused, "a gun detachment without even a straggling cavalryman for support." As the gunners blazed away at the Federal flank, they needed only to point their rifle in the right direction and they were virtually sure to cause damage somewhere along the enemy line. Rosser told Sergeant Pleasants, "You can't help hitting something anywhere you fire up that way." Cannoneer Wills Lee boasted that the Richmond gunners "fired shot, shell and canister point blank down [the enemy's] flank."[63]

The Confederate artillerymen were deployed in the open, and Pleasants wrote that "the enemy could see us from our shoe-soles up," yet the Southerners apparently suffered no casualties until their ammunition ran out and the detachment was in the act of withdrawing. Their luck quickly changed, however, for the Richmond Howitzers eventually lost nine out of fourteen men, eleven out of twelve horses, and one limber chest blown up before withdrawing under Pelham's orders. With such losses in horses, the gun had to be left behind and was temporarily captured. Some of Rosser's dismounted cavalrymen pushed the Federals back from their briefly held trophy, thereby permitting the Richmond Howitzer artillerists to bring the cannon off by hand.[64]

Steve Dandridge, a member of the Rockbridge Artillery, accompanied the gun from their battery that went forward with Pelham and Rosser. He wrote that Pelham was "as gallant a fellow as I ever saw," and indicated that Rosser "was with us all through the fight." Pelham told the gunners that he would ask them to fight in the advanced position until they suffered a fatality, whereupon he would relieve the battery. The unit suffered many more killed than that, however. "Our company has been terribly cut up," Dandridge wrote to his mother. The battery "lost 6 killed, and ten or twelve badly wounded." Dandridge reported that the heavy losses impacted the spirits of the men, and that the face of every man had "a look of sorrow" in the battery bivouac.[65]

After William Franklin's Federal attack was repulsed, many of the gun crews on Prospect Hill were relieved. The portion of the Rockbridge Artillery not already serving with Pelham was one of the detachments called from their reserve position. While enroute to Prospect Hill, artillerist Ham Chamberlayne met the men, telling them of the extreme losses suffered throughout the day at the very destination where they were headed. Nearly everyone who spotted Chamberlayne on that day noted his peculiar headgear, as he had a handkerchief wrapped around his head. Most accounts also noted his animated behavior. One of the batterymen, Carter N. B. Minor, described his manner as "frantic" and "most unbecoming a good judicious officer." But Minor conceded that despite his appearance and demeanor, "he could do good service on the field." Dr. A. J. Hayslett, who was accompanying Captain Poague and did not know the identity of the peculiar officer crowned with the handkerchief concluded: "Well, that fellow must be crazy, don't you think?" to which Pogue replied, "He's alright, that's Ham Chamberlayne," apparently appreciating the unusual head gear as normal behavior, considering the man.[66]

Since most of the rifled pieces from the artillery reserve had already been sent to Pelham earlier in the day, the weapons sent to Prospect Hill were primarily smoothbore guns. Poague's two large 20-pounder Parrott rifles were the exception, so Jackson gave them special instructions to fire upon an enemy battery. Poague's shots seemingly stirred up a hornet's nest, attracting a fearsome return fire during what had been a relatively quiet period on Prospect Hill.

Minor observed that the Federals "had been firing on the point for hours, & had the range perfectly," whereas the newcomers upon the scene had had no opportunity to establish proper barrel elevation or the timing for fuses, and accordingly suffered severely. While Minor and Ned Alexander were setting the fuses at one of the gun's limber chests, an enemy shell landed near, stunning Minor and badly injuring Alexander. Sparks from the explosion ignited one or two cartridges where the artillerymen were working, charring Alexander's face and beard and injuring one of his arms so badly as to require amputation.[67] Minor later witnessed Lt. Baxter McCorkle draw his pistol to end the misery of a mangled horse that had wandered in amongst the battery. A moment later, the junior lieutenant himself was dead as well.[68]

Poague's uneven contest was ended when Lt. Col. Lewis Minor Coleman ordered the crew to cease firing. Coleman, second in command of Brown's reserve artillery battalion, had been a professor of Latin at the University of Virginia before the war. His half-brother, Vivian Minor Fleming, served in the 2nd Richmond Howitzers, which had not received any time to prepare a morning meal before it was detached for service with Pelham. Coleman had given his brother a couple of biscuits as his section moved to the front. Fleming would later reflect, "that was the last time I saw my brother again till I saw him. . .lying upon his death bed." A bullet or shell fragment struck Coleman beneath his knee "when in the act of pointing one of his guns," but he considered it so trifling that he stayed on the battlefield until the action had ended, and was only then taken to a field hospital. He later died of "virulent erysipelas." Coleman was the ranking Confederate artillery officer to fall at Fredericksburg.[69]

The aggressive Thomas Jackson planned a twilight attack for the evening of December 13, and Confederate artillery was called upon to shell the Federal position in advance of the infantry movement. The response from Federal ordnance was so powerful, however, that Jackson cancelled his order for the assault. Most of Jackson's men dreaded the idea of the proposed attack and were quite delighted over the change of plans. The rescinded orders allowed the soldiers to regroup and take care of other unfinished business brought about by the day's action.

After dark, Minor and some others from the Rockbridge Artillery returned to Prospect Hill to retrieve a caisson they had been unable to remove due to the loss of horses. Part of the mission included retrieving the body of a fallen gunner, Randolph Fairfax. His corpse was placed upon the caisson and steadied by two of his comrades as the party headed back to camp. The wound that killed Fairfax apparently caused little deformity to his body. Minor observed his "noble, beautiful face, & lonely still, even in death." As they buried him, Minor solemnly wrote, their "silent prayers were the only funeral service."[70]

The Southern artillerists were justifiably pleased with their performance. The Confederate gunners assessed their day as one in which they were in the thick of the most furious fighting, suffered very heavy casualties, provided excellent service, and were allowed to freely perform their specialty. "It was a severe day on all the artillery," Capt. David Watson of the 2nd Richmond Howitzers wrote just four days after the battle, "and my battery formed no exception to the rule." Indeed all of the artillery experienced peril, as A. P. Hill teasingly suggested in his report: "Pegram, as usual, with McIntosh to help him, managed to find the hottest place, though perhaps Davidson might have been willing to exchange positions with them."[71]

"To-day I have been in the hottest fight I have ever heard of," wrote a member of the Pee Dee Artillery about his experiences on Prospect Hill. "From ten o'clock this morning till an hour or two since shot and shell, and Minie balls, having been perfectly hailing around me." The same gunner concluded, "All the other fights crowded into one would hardly make anything to be compared to to-day's fight."[72]

Captain David G. McIntosh, commander of the Pee Dee Artillery and an attached section on Prospect Hill, was informed by Pelham on the day after the battle that J. E. B. Stuart had been "highly pleased" with the service provided by his battery. The captain concluded, "so I am disposed to brag a little," as he wrote to his mother.[73]

"It was here for the first time that the Confederate artillery was systematically massed for battle," said Armistead L. Long about the successes of the battalion system. William White observed: "The loss amongst our artillerists has been much greater than in any previous engagement, but that is easily explained, for it was managed by 'Chiefs of Artillery' and not infantry brigadiers, as is usually the case, and for that reason it was the more effective."[74]

The effectiveness of the Southern artillery on the Confederate right is beyond dispute. The early morning action of Pelham's solitary gun was more than an amazing feat of daring—as the Federal decision to detain Doubleday's 6,000-man division from participating in the subsequent attack demonstrates. The significance of Pelham's exploit takes on added meaning when one ponders what the Federals might have accomplished with that body of men added to the numbers exploiting the breach in the Confederate line.

The initial positions of the Confederate artillery proved to be expertly selected by the manner in which the cannon, with little assistance needed from the infantry, brought the divisions of Meade and Gibbon to a standstill. The bold placement of Brockenbrough's guns where they could not expect to remain for the duration of the battle was the key in enabling the Southern gunners to cover every piece of ground the Yankee infantry had to traverse.

The halt in the first attack and subsequent withdrawal of Meade and Gibbon—which allowed Federal artillerymen another chance to soften the Confederate line—came at a time when Burnside estimated that Franklin's assault should have been well under way. In accordance with his plans to launch a diversionary attack *after* his primary attack had become general, Burnside ordered a series of attacks lasting the remainder of the day against Marye's Heights and the stone wall that lined the Sunken Road below. The longer these attacks went on, the more lopsided the battle became, as Federal dead and wounded piled up beneath the heights. Had the attacks against Marye's Heights been launched later in the day—at the time when Meade and Gibbon had indeed closed with the Rebel infantry—the Federal casualty lists might not have been as long. Burnside presumed that when Meade and Gibbon went forward they would engage the Confederate infantry; the Confederate artillery proved his reckoning to be wrong.

The renewal of the Meade–Gibbon assault occurred during a time when Brockenbrough's guns were no longer in their advanced position. The effectiveness of Brockenbrough's guns in the first attack became obvious during the renewal of the contest. Without those twelve guns firing from in front of the railroad, the Federals reached their first objective and penetrated the Confederate line. Once Meade and Gibbon wrestled Lane's North Carolinians from their position, the Federals stood on the verge of rolling up one of the weakest portions of the Confederate line. Holding the position defending Hood's right was Davidson's Confederate artillery group. These gunners held their ground and called for double canister—the round indicative of the closest kind of combat.

The Confederate gunners proved that they deserved the newly-granted authority of the battalion system. They chose their ground wisely and did not hesitate to place their guns squarely in harm's path when the situation called for it. The infantrymen would continue to be the backbone of the army, even after the advent of the artillery battalion system, but the contributions of the artillery on the Confederate right had a significant impact on the outcome of the Battle of Fredericksburg.

Endnotes:

1. William T. Poague, *Gunner With Stonewall* (Wilmington, 1987), p. 50.

2. Captain Carter M. Braxton letter to his sisters, Oct. 11, 1862, Ann Brown Memorial Collection, Brown University.

3. Pegram's group, from right to left, consisted of a two-gun section under Lt. James B. Ellett's from the Crenshaw (Virginia) Artillery, and four guns of Pegram's own Purcell (Virginia) Artillery. McIntosh's group, from right to left, contained four guns from McIntosh's own Pee Dee (South Carolina) Artillery, a two-gun section under Lt. V. J. Clutter from Johnson's (Virginia) Battery, and a two-gun section under Lt. J. R. Potts from Latham's (North Carolina) Battery. David Gregg McIntosh, Manuscript, "A Ride on Horseback in the Summer of 1910 over Some of the Battlefields of the Great Civil War with Some Notes of the Battles," Southern Historical Collection, University of North Carolina.

4. Ibid.

5. Davidson's initial nine guns came from his own Letcher (Virginia) Artillery; part of the Fredericksburg (Virginia) Artillery, also known as Braxton's Battery, under Lt. Edward A. Marye; the Hampden (Virginia) Artillery under Capt. William H. Caskie; and the Lee (Virginia) Artillery or Raine's Battery, under Lt. Charles W. Statham. The Letcher and Fredericksburg Artillery belonged to Maj. Gen. A. P. Hill's Division; the Hampden and Lee Artillery belonged to Brig. Gen. William B. Taliaferro's Division. Specific alignment of the artillery at the Bernard Cabins is not known. The gun compliment

included six rifles, two 12-pounder Napoleons, and one 6-pounder field gun. United States War Department, War of the Rebellion: *A Compilation of the Official Records of the Union and Confederate Armies* 128 vols. (Washington, D.C., 1890-1901), Series 1, vol. 21, p. 637, hereinafter cited as *OR*.

Latimer's five guns included a two-rifle section from his own Courtney (Virginia) Artillery commanded by Lt. W. A. Tanner, and three rifles from the Chesapeake (Maryland) Artillery, also known as Brown's Battery, under Lt. John E. Plater. *OR* 21, p. 668.

6. Charles W. Turner, *Captain Greenlee Davidson, C. S. A.: Diary and Letters* (Verona, 1975), p. 63.

7. Ibid.

8. *OR* 21, p. 636.

9. Ibid., pp. 636-637. While Crutchfield states that the artillery position being discussed was 200 yards in front of Davidson's guns and beyond the railroad. Davidson estimated that the railroad was 300 yards from his front. Davidson's appraisal of distances seems quite accurate, and a more reasonable estimate of the distance between Davidson and the group placed under Brockenbrough would be about 400 yards.

10. Brockenbrough's group contained details from Carpenter's (Virginia) Battery, under Lt. George McKendree; the Danville (Virginia) Artillery, under Capt. G. W. Wooding; and the remainder of the Fredericksburg Artillery not already serving with Davidson. The compliment was made up of six rifles, three 12-pounder Napoleons, and three 6-pounder guns. McKendree's guns appear to have been on the left of the line, but the exact order of the units or number of guns from each unit are not known. *OR* 21, p. 636. The Fredericksburg Artillery was divided between the two groupings under Davidson and Brockenbrough. Ironically, the Confederates posted cannon on the ridge named for the battery commander's family, but neither Lieutenant Edward "Ned" Marye nor other members of the unit would have the chance to literally defend their homes—duty required them to be some three miles south of Fredericksburg.

11. The nature of the role of cavalry, with detached units often the rule, coupled with the absence of accounts dealing with the horse artillery, leaves much doubt about the specific participation by batteries of the horse artillery. The most conspicuous role played by a battery under Pelham's command in the approaching Fredericksburg battle would be Henry's (Virginia) Battery, under Capt. Mathis Winston Henry. Moorman's (Virginia) Battery, under Capt. M. N. Moorman was at hand, but was not engaged. A footnote in casualty returns contains a notation for Breathed's (Virginia) Battery, under Capt. James Breathed, which reads: "One man killed in Breathed's battery not accounted for." Chew's (Virginia) Battery, commanded by R. P. Chew, and Hart's (South Carolina) Battery, lead by Capt. J. F. Hart, round out the units assigned to the Stuart Horse Artillery, which may have been at Fredericksburg. *OR* 21, p. 558.

12. The units from Brown's Battalion included: two Parrotts from the Rockbridge (Virginia) Artillery (Poague's Battery), under Lt. Archibald Graham; two rifles from the 3rd Richmond Howitzers under Lt. James S. Utz; two 10-pounder Parrotts and one bronze rifle from 2nd Richmond Howitzers, Capt. Watson commanding; and one 3-inch rifle from the Powhatan Artillery, Capt. Willis S. Dance, commanding. *OR* 21, p. 638.

The units from Jubal Early's Division included: three guns from the Louisiana Guards, commanded by Capt. Louis E. D'Aquin; and the Staunton (Virginia) Artillery, under Lt. Asher W. Garber. Ibid., p. 669.

13. Ibid., p. 631.

14. Lieutenant R. Channing Price, letter to his mother Dec. 17, 1862, R. Channing Price Papers, University of North Carolina.

15. William S. White, *Contributions to a History of the Richmond Howitzer Battalion, Pamphlet No. 2, by Third Richmond Howitzers, First Virginia Artillery* (Richmond, 1883), p. 147.

16. *OR* 21, p. 633.

17. Turner, *Davidson*, p. 63.

18. Carter Nelson Berkley Minor, manuscript, James Fontaine Minor Papers, University of Virginia; John William Ford Hatton, manuscript, Library of Congress.

19. George W. Shreve, "Reminiscences of the Stuart Horse Artillery," a typescript in the R. Preston Chew Papers, Jefferson County Museum, West Virginia. The closest weather station to Fredericksburg in operation during the war was at Georgetown, about fifty miles north of Fredericksburg. On December 11, 1863 the temperature at 7:00 a.m. was 24 degrees; on December 13, the temperature at the same time of day was 34 degrees. So just two days before the main battle the thermometer read well below the freezing mark, and soldiers readily noted the warming trend leading up to (and extending beyond) the Battle of Fredericksburg.

20. Price letter, December 17, 1862.

21. Shreve, "Reminiscences of the Stuart Horse Artillery."

22. Ibid.

23. John Esten Cooke, *Philadelphia Weekly Times*, April 26, 1879, Price letter, December 17, 1862.

24. Shreve, "Reminiscences of the Stuart Horse Artillery."

25. Cooke, *Philadelphia Weekly Times*, April 26, 1879.

26. Heros Von Borke, *Memoirs of the Confederate War for Independence* (Dayton, 1985), p. 118.

27. Ibid., p. 118. John Cheves Haskell, letter to John Warwick Daniel, May 12, 1906, John Warwick Daniel Papers, Duke University; *OR* 21, p. 558.

28. Price letter, December 17, 1862.

29. Ibid.; *OR* 21, p. 547. Cooke, *Philadelphia Weekly Times*, April 26, 1879.

30. *OR* 21, p. 631; *London Times*, January 13, 1863; Cooke, *Philadelphia Weekly Times*, April 26, 1879.

31. Frank A. O'Reilly, *"Stonewall" Jackson at Fredericksburg: The Battle of Prospect Hill, December 13, 1862* (Lynchburg, 1993), pp. 50-51.

32. Letter from "Ben" to father, in the *Charleston Daily Courier*, December 30, 1862.

33. McIntosh, "A Ride on Horseback"; *Charleston Daily Courier*.

34. Peter S. Carmichael, *The Purcell, Crenshaw and Letcher Artillery* (Lynchburg, 1990) pp. 102-104; John O'Farrell diary, Museum of the Confederacy; William Ellis Jones diary, University of Michigan.

35. "Eulogy of David G. McIntosh," Pegram-Johnson-McIntosh Papers, Virginia Historical Society; Carmichael, *The Purcell, Crenshaw and Letcher Artillery*, pp. 104-105.

36. Minor Manuscript.

37. McIntosh, "A Ride on Horseback."

38. *OR* 21, 21, p. 631.

39. *Report of the Joint Committee on the Conduct of the War*, vol. 1 (Washington, D.C., 1863), p. 653.

40. *OR* 21, 21, p. 679.

41. Ibid., p. 637.

42. Ibid., pp. 637, 677. See also Jennings Cropper Wise, *The Long Arm of Lee: The History of the Artillery of the Army of Northern Virginia* (New York, 1959), pp. 383-385, for additional information and insights.

43. Ibid., p. 637.

44. Ibid., 668; Turner, *Davidson*, p. 65. Latimer was mortally wounded on July 2, 1863, during the second day's fighting at Gettysburg. One subordinate wrote of Latimer: "I believe he is the very best Arty. Capt. in Genl. Lee's Army and would make the best Maj. and I know we have worse Generals by far than he wd. make." Quoted from Robert K. Krick, *Lee's Colonels* (Dayton, 1991), p. 231.

45. Ibid., p. 64.

46. Ibid.

47. *OR* 21, 21, p. 637.

48. Carmichael, *The Purcell, Crenshaw and Letcher Artillery*, p. 149; *OR* 21, p. 637.

49. *Charleston Daily Courier.*

50. Ibid.

51. Robert J. Driver, Jr., *The 1st and 2nd Rockbridge Artillery* (Lynchburg, 1988), pp. 34-36.

52. Ibid., p. 36.

53. Vivian Minor Fleming, *Reminiscence*, Fredericksburg and Spotsylvania National Military Park, bound volume 23.

54. *OR* 21, p. 679.

55. George H. Mills, *History of the 16th North Carolina Regiment (Originally 6th N.C. Regiment) in the Civil War* (Rutherfordton, 1901), p. 28.

56. Turner, *Davidson*, p. 64.

57. Ibid.

58. Ibid., p. 66.

59. Ibid.

60. Ibid., p. 67.

61. Price letter, December 17, 1862.

62. Reuben B. Pleasants, *Contributions to a History of the Richmond Howitzer Battalion, Pamphlet No. 3* (Richmond, 1884), p. 59.

63. Ibid., pp. 59-60; Wills Lee, typescript, FSNMP, bound volume 138.

64. Pleasants, *Richmond Howitzer Battalion*, p. 60.

65. Steve Dandridge letter to Mother, December 19, 1862, Bedinger-Dandridge Family Papers, Duke University.

66. Minor Manuscript; Pogue, *Gunner With Stonewall*, p. 55.

67. Minor Manuscript.

68. Ibid.

69. Fleming, *Reminiscence*.

70. Minor Manuscript.

71. John Lipscomb Johnson, *The University Memorial Biographical Sketches* (Baltimore, 1871), p. 575; OR 21, p. 648.

72. *Charleston Daily Courier*.

73. McIntosh, "A Ride on Horseback."

74. Armistead L. Long, *Philadelphia Saturday*, January 16, 1886, vol. 9, No. 48; Pleasants, *Richmond Howitzer Battalion*, p. 148.

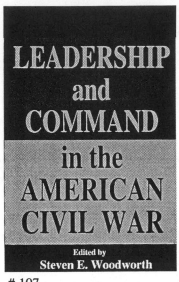

107

Leadership and Command
in the
American Civil War

edited by
Steven E. Woodworth
(author of the new *Davis & Lee at War*)

- Five original essays

- 14 custom strategic & tactical maps

- Photos, index

- Cloth, d.j., 248pp. $24.95

- ISBN 1-882810-00-7

This compendium of carefully-selected essays proves again that there are a multitude of subjects and personalities awaiting original study and thoughtful contemplation. These articles shatter several Civil War misconceptions. Incls. 14 original maps by cartographer Mark A. Moore.

Ole Joe in Virginia: Gen. Joseph E. Johnston's 1861-1862
Period of Command in the East, by Richard M. McMurry

The Detachment of Longstreet Considered: Braxton Bragg, James Longstreet, and the
Chattanooga Campaign, by Edward Carr Franks

A Failure of Command? A Reassessment of the Generalship of Maj. Gen. Edwin V. Sumner and
the Federal II Corps at Antietam, by Marion V. Armstrong

The Seeds of Disaster: The Generalship of George E. Pickett
After Gettysburg, by L esley J. Gordon

On Smaller Fields: General P. G. T. Beauregard and the
Bermuda Hundred Campaign, by Steven E. Woodworth

Savas Woodbury Publishers
1475 S. Bascom Ave., Suite 204, Campbell, CA 95008
Order toll free: 1-800-848-6585 (ask for our free catalog!)

The 20th Massachusetts Infantry and the Street Fight for Fredericksburg

Richard F. Miller and Robert F. Mooney

> When we got into our quarters, we sat down and talked the matter over. Well we knew what was in store for us, we knew that we were to make an attempt to cross the river and gain the city and take the heights beyond, and knowing how strongly fortified the rebs were we knew what a reception we should get, and that many of us would never see the light of another day. However we were soldiers and must take our chances.
>
> —Private Josiah Fitch Murphey, Company I,
> 20th Massachusetts Volunteer Infantry.[1]

At 3:00 a.m. on December 11, 1862, engineers from the Army of the Potomac began unloading pontoon trains at three points along a two mile stretch of the Rappahannock River. The northernmost point would be the site of two parallel pontoon bridges called the Upper Bridge. Wooden planks laid over the sides of long, narrow punts would connect the plain at the foot of Stafford Heights forward of the Lacy House to the northern section of the town of Fredericksburg. The 50th New York Engineers under Maj. Ira Spaulding was responsible for its construction.

The second bridge, which would be known as the Middle Bridge, would be laid approximately one mile south of the Upper Bridge. Its pontoons would connect with the southern fringe of the town. The 15th New York Engineers under Lt. Michael H. McGrath was assigned the task of its construction.

The southernmost bridge was, predictably, called the Lower Bridge. It was located about a mile south of the Middle Bridge and about a quarter mile south of a stream known as Deep Run. A regular army engineer battalion under the command of Lt. Charles E. Cross oversaw its construction. Unlike the Upper and Middle Bridges which faced the houses, barns and warehouses of the town, the Lower Bridge essentially connected two fields and confronted few entrenchments. As a result, this bridge would be constructed on time and with little opposition.

Braving 25 degree temperatures, snow covered ground and ice on the river as thick as six inches in places, the engineers began their work in darkness, trying their best to muffle the sounds of construction. While the impending attack on Fredericksburg was an open secret in both the Northern and Southern press, the exact time and place of Maj. Gen. Ambrose Burnside's strike was presumably unknown. Well known to every Union picket on the Rappahannock River, however, was the presence of enemy troops and fortifications just 400 feet away on the opposite bank.

One member of Burnside's Army of the Potomac, Massachusetts private Josiah F. Murphey, described these fortifications:

> We were camped about three fourths of a mile from the river back of a small town called Falmouth and would frequently make a trip to the river to see what the rebs were doing on the other side. We could see that they were building strong lines of works. . . .[On Marye's Heights] the rebs built their lines of works three or four of them, one overlooking the other like seats in a theatre, only farther apart. Each line could get in its work by firing over the heads of those in front, a little risky, perhaps, but then they take risks in battle. The rebs also built a line of breastworks in front of the city next to the river where they were to make their first resistance.[2]

As the engineers began their work in the small hours of December 11th, fortunately, and for a time, a thick winter fog arose from the river and concealed them from their Confederate adversaries. The evening before, Maj. George Nelson Macy, acting commander of the 20th Massachusetts, had received his orders from Col. Norman J. Hall, commanding the Third Brigade of Oliver O. Howard's Second Division, Darius N. Couch's Second Federal Corps. The Second Corps had been assigned to Maj. Gen. Edwin Vose Sumner's Right Grand

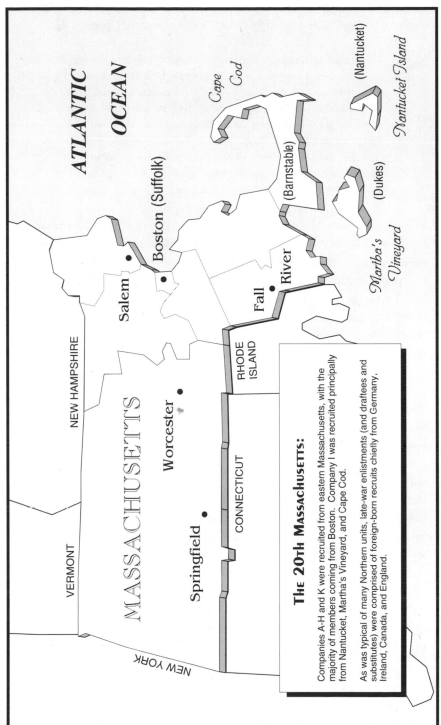

ATLANTIC OCEAN

(Nantucket)

Nantucket Island

Cape Cod

Boston (Suffolk)

(Barnstable)

Salem

Fall River

(Dukes)

Martha's Vineyard

NEW HAMPSHIRE

RHODE ISLAND

Worcester

MASSACHUSETTS

CONNECTICUT

VERMONT

Springfield

NEW YORK

THE 20TH MASSACHUSETTS:

Companies A–H and K were recruited from eastern Massachusetts, with the majority of members coming from Boston. Company I was recruited principally from Nantucket, Martha's Vineyard, and Cape Cod.

As was typical of many Northern units, late-war enlistments (and draftees and substitutes) were comprised of foreign-born recruits chiefly from Germany, Ireland, Canada, and England.

Mark A. Moore

Division. Writing two weeks later, Macy explained how the 20th Massachusetts had been selected to lead the Right Grand Division over the Upper Bridge:

> I will state first, though, that [at] a council of war, held the night previous, Gen. Couch was given the advance. Gen. Couch turned to Gen. Howard and said, 'Your division will have the advance.' Gen. Howard turned to Col. Hall and said, 'Your brigade will have the honor of leading the Army of the Potomac across the river.' Col. Hall gave the 20th the front, and told me that I should lead the Brigade. Well, I felt proud of that—felt ready for anything—felt sure that I have penned my last letter—however, I felt that I could lead the 20th, and I knew they would follow.[3]

Brigaded with Macy's men were the 7th Michigan (Hall's former regiment), the 19th Massachusetts, the 42nd New York (known as the Tammany Regiment), the 59th New York, and the 127th Pennsylvania.

With the 20th Massachusetts in the van, Sumner's Right Grand Division would cross at the Upper Bridges, while Maj. Gen. Joseph Hooker's Center Grand Division would drive across on the Middle span. While Sumner's and Hooker's men secured their sectors, Maj. Gen. William B. Franklin's Left Grand Division would cross at the Lower Bridge.

Central to Burnside's plan of securing the far bank of the Rappahannock were the 30 to 50 foot high bluffs of Stafford Heights, which ran along the banks of the river opposite Fredericksburg (on the Federal side of the river) for some five miles. Union artillery chief Brig. Gen. Henry J. Hunt had posted 183 guns on these heights, training them on the town of Fredericksburg and the hills just beyond. The artillery would have three missions in supporting the upcoming advance: drive the entrenched Confederates from the hills west of town; prevent enemy forces from massing on the open plains opposite the Lower Bridge; and most important to the engineers and the troops who would cross over on the temporary bridges, suppress enemy opposition to the construction of the bridges and subsequent troop movements. In the words of one student of the battle, Burnside's plan "confidently assumed" that the artillery could do the job.[4]

About 3:00 a.m. on the 11th, Murphey and his comrades were recalled from picket duty and ordered to fall in with the balance of the regiment near the Lacy House. As Major Macy remembered it, at about daylight:

> . . .the 20th led the Brigade and we marched to the river. The
> cannonade had already opened, and never was there a more beauti-
> ful sight than that morning as we marched forth to battle. The moon
> was just setting and the sun rising, while a thick mist enveloped
> everything. It was grand indeed, and never did troops feel in better
> spirits.[5]

Another member of the 20th Massachusetts, Lt. Henry Ropes of Company
K, wrote to his brother John a week later describing the early morning march
into position to cross the Rappahannock River:

> . . .at 6 A.M. [the 20th Massachusetts] marched down to a point
> about opposite the Northern part of the city. It was still very dark,
> the valley of the river was filled with smoke from our batteries
> along the bank, and the noise was tremendous. We staid on an open
> plain which was filled with troops. Our Brigade was to cross first,
> the 7th [Michigan] leading as skirmishers.[6]

Construction on each bridge was well underway by the time the cold
winter's darkness had given way to the early light of the new day. Before 6:00
a.m., all bridges were somewhere between one-half and two-thirds completed.
Jutting into the icy Rappahannock, the engineers beavered away on the bridgeheads, concealed from the Confederates by the fog. By the time 6:00 a.m.
arrived, however, the growing daylight thinned the mist and the engineers working on the Upper and Middle Bridges became visible to the sharpshooters of
Brig. Gen. William Barksdale's Mississippians and the 8th Florida Infantry,
brigaded together and deployed among the buildings of Fredericksburg for one
purpose: to prevent or delay the construction of the bridges.

As Confederate sharpshooters killed and wounded Federal engineers in a
lethal dawn volley, the first of several flaws which marked Burnside's plans to
convey his army across the river became evident. The Union commander had
failed to anticipate that enemy sharpshooters—concealed behind fences and
breastworks, in cellars and houses and the warehouses of the town—could turn
simple plank bridges into bottlenecks of death. By aiming squarely at the un-
armed engineers on the bridgeheads, Barksdale's men seriously threatened the
advance of two-thirds of the Union army.

The luck of the 50th New York Engineers was the first to run out. At 6:00
a.m., Major Spaulding reported that, "the enemy opened a galling fire upon us
at the upper bridges, from the houses near the shore and from behind walls and

fences, killing one captain and 2 men."[7] As a result of this deadly fire, Spaulding's men were forced to temporarily abandon work on the unfinished bridge. As Lt. Ropes described matters, efforts to protect the engineers were futile:

> The river here is about as wide as Pemberton Square [in Boston] is long, and the bank's high and especially steep on our side. The 7th Michigan and the 19th [Massachsuetts] were deployed as skirmishers to protect the laborers on the bridge, but they could not do so, for the smoke and fog were very thick.[8]

Major Macy's recollections of the affair reflected both regimental morale and the growing frustration with Confederate resistance:

> Col. Hall was ordered to put two regiments on the river bank to pick off the enemy. He put the 7th Mich. and 19th there. He told me that, although these two regiments were put in this position to my front, that I need not look so disappointed about it, as he should put the 20th where they were promised and where the best troops would be needed—time passed on—our guns opened upon the houses occupied by the shooters and battered many down, but the enemy laughed at this and stood deliberately before us and ran from wall to wall.[9]

At the Middle Bridge, the engineers fared somewhat better, at least for a time. By 8:15 a.m., as the final section of the bridge was being laid, Confederate pickets emerged from the houses and barns in which they had been hidden, "rapidly ran forward 20 paces, peered over the bank, and ascertaining the position of our landing, hastily retired behind the houses." Two enemy companies then appeared and fired on the hapless engineers, wounding six and piercing the pontoon boats "in many places." Here too, construction was temporarily abandoned.[10]

At the Lower Bridge, which faced an empty plain and only token opposition, the engineers completed their demanding task by 9:00 a.m. Because of the delays occasioned by enemy resistance at the Middle and Upper Bridges, however, and wishing a simultaneous movement of his whole army, Burnside delayed Franklin's crossing until 4:00 p.m. that afternoon.

The attempt of those Union sharpshooters stationed at both the Upper and Middle Bridges to silence their Confederate counterparts by trading shot for shot was complicated by more than battle smoke and lingering mists. The Confederate "killing fields," as one soldier described them, were only 80 feet

Bvt. Maj. Gen. George Nelson Macy,
ca. 1865. Macy was Nantucket's highest ranking officer of the Civil War.

Courtesy of the Houghton Library, Harvard University.

Two views of **Josiah Fitch Murphey,** the first after his recovery from typhoid fever in August 1863 (left); and below, at age 74 (ca. 1917) in his G.A.R. uniform. Note the facial scar just beneath his eye that he received during the fight for the streets of Fredericksburg. Murphey marked the photograph to indicate the wound. *Photos courtesy of Francis W. Pease and the authors, respectively.*

A postwar image of **Maj. John W. Summer-hayes,** ca. 1890, as a lieutenant colonel in the Regular Army. *Courtesy of the Nantucket Historical Association.*

from their shore (about where the unfinished bridgeheads were abandoned), while Union sharpshooters (from the far bank) had to hit a well-concealed enemy at distances of more than 400 feet.

When the Federal infantry failed to suppress the enemy, the work of dislodgement fell to the artillery. Colonel Charles H. Tompkins, commanding the First Rhode Island Light Artillery as well as all artillery assigned to support the Right Center Division—Hunt had deployed his artillery into Right, Right Center, Left Center and Left Divisions, so named for their positions on Stafford Heights—commenced a minuet that would consume most of the day. His batteries opened "a rapid fire for a few moments; then ceased, to enable the engineers to continue their work."[11]

The engineers had no sooner returned to their work than the Confederate sharpshooters opened fire again. The sharp staccata of the small arms fire caused Tompkins' batteries, whose guns bristled over the Upper and Middle Bridges, to open fire once more at 8:00 a.m. This second barrage once again silenced the Confederates, and the hapless engineers bravely returned to their deadly labors. Almost immediately the Confederates returned and resumed their deadly game with the skill of well-trained technicians.

Why wasn't the Federal artillery effective at this stage of the engagement? Its ineffectual implementation was primarily the result of three problems encountered by the Union gunners. First, and most easily addressed, shells from the 12-pounder guns "burst short," reported Colonel Tompkins of the First Rhode Island Light Artillery, "thereby endangering our men."[12] This galling dilemma was at least partially solved by switching to less effective solid shot. The second problem, a much more serious matter, was that Stafford Heights was too high relative to the opposite bank—the immediate area along and behind which the Rebels were concealed—to allow General Hunt's guns to sufficiently depress their barrels to hit riverside targets. Hunt solved this problem by withdrawing thirty-six light 12-pounder guns from the heights and redeploying them directly on the river bank. Twenty-four of these pieces were posted behind the Upper Bridge, and the remaining twelve behind the Middle Bridge.

It was the third problem, however, and one that was essentially unsolveable, that posed the greatest threat to the Union advance. It was the same problem that would be faced in future wars by armies that blithely assumed that the destruction of buildings harboring an enemy would result in their destruction. As the Germans would discover at Leningrad and the Russians at Berlin in 1945, artillery alone could not successfully empty a city of its defenders. December 11th is only ten days before the Winter Solstice, and the short day was mostly devoted to futile attempts by Hunt's artillery to blast Barksdale's men from the town. One Confederate officer counted nine separate artillery barrages, each followed by the Federal engineers attempts to return to the bridgeheads.[13] However many their number, these barrages were also intended, as ordered by Burnside, to indiscriminately shell the town. Beginning at 12:30 p.m., the bombardment lasted two hours and fired an estimated 9,000 rounds into the historic American city. Yet General Hunt noted that even after this tremendous attack, which rendered the town "untenable by any considerable body. . .a few hundred sharpshooters, scattered among the cellars, in ditches, and behind stone walls, drove them [the engineers] from the bridges."[14]

The reasons why the artillery proved so ineffectual were described by Brig. Gen. Daniel P. Woodbury, Burnside's chief engineer, in his tour of Fredericksburg following the city's capture:

> I found a loop-holed block-house, uninjured by our artillery, directly opposite our upper bridges, and only a few yards from their southern abutment. I also found in the neighborhood a rifle-pit behind a stone wall, some 200 feet long, and cellars inclosed by heavy walls, where the enemy could load and fire in almost perfect safety. There were many other secure shelters.[15]

As the generals schemed and the artillery dueled with the Confederate infantry strategically lodged amidst the growing rubble, the 20th Massachusetts watched and waited near the riverbank. Lieutenant Ropes vividly described the scene from his perspective on the far shore:

> After a little time the guns were directed to the City to clear out the Rebel sharpshooters, and the bombardment lasted steadily till about 4 P.M. The City was now on fire in 3 places, and this smoke added to the darkness through which our guns incessantly flashed. We were close to the batteries. The sound was tremendous. We had now lain all day here and still nothing was done. . . .[16]

As daylight slipped away it was abundantly clear to almost everyone involved that something new would have to be tried in order to force a crossing en masse. And Gen. Henry J. Hunt had an idea.

*   *   *

Well they opened fire agane and Set [a] lot Houses A Fire but it
Would Not Work. So the General Cold for Volinteers and Cornel
Hall Volunteered to Cross With his Brigade. . .this Was Cold the
Forlone Hope and they Sayed the Cuntry Would Never Forgit us.

—Private Daniel McAdams, Company I,
20th Massachusetts Volunteer Infantry.[17]

When the artillery proved ineffective against the Confederates, another idea had to be implemented in order to cross the river. As General Hunt tersely recalled in his after action report:

About 2:30 o'clock, I proposed to fill the bateaux, not yet in their places in the bridges, with infantry, to make a dash to the opposite side, while the troops should land and attack the enemy in his cover, to row the pontoons to their places and complete the bridges. This plan was adopted.[18]

In fact, the difficulties Hunt experienced in obtaining consent for the plan typified the weak and uncertain leadership that plagued the Union command.[19] After the grand bombardment of Fredericksburg failed to dislodge the Confederate sharpshooters but worked to infuriate the tens of thousands of Confederates who were watching as the historic city tumbled into rubble, a frustrated Burnside sent for Hunt. "The army is held by the throat by a few sharpshooters!" he shouted at Hunt, whereupon the artillery chief proposed his plan to send 1,000 men in boats to drive the Confederates from the town. Burnside at first gave conditional assent: if Hunt could persuade General Woodbury to support the plan, he would issue the order. Hunt obtained Woodbury's agreement, and returned with the chief engineer to Burnside's headquarters for the order.

It was at this point that Burnside began to hedge a bit, because he did not want to accept responsibility for so risky a mission. Instead, he interjected a new condition: if Hunt could convince the infantry to make the waterborne assault, he would consent to the plan. Hunt and Woodbury returned to the river and literally buttonholed the first infantry commander they found—Colonel Norman J. Hall—who immediately agreed to move forward against the enemy.

One more significant obstacle in the chain of command remained. Major General Edwin V. Sumner, the commander of the Second Corps, may have been feeling miffed at having been left out of the planning. When he learned of the plan, he ordered Colonel Hall to suspend preparations for the proposed assault.

Hall obeyed his superior and it appeared that Hunt's plan would not be implemented after all.

When Norman J. Hall was appointed to command the Third Brigade, he was succeeded as colonel of the 7th Michigan by Henry Baxter. It was Baxter who, defying Sumner's order, declared he was willing to go without reservation. Officers of the 89th New York—which was to cross in boats at the Middle Bridge—together with the 19th and 20th Massachusetts supported Baxter's impromptu bravado and threw in with the 7th's commander. Fortified by his subordinate's stiff backbone, Hall decided to join in Baxter's resolve. Without regard to Sumner's objections, he issued a solitary order: the 7th Michigan, followed by the 19th Massachusetts, was to board the unused pontoon scows and row across the river, form on the opposite bank, and drive the sharpshooters from their perches.

Hall arranged for the engineers to line up the boats along the banks and also received their promise to row and steer them across the river. As Union batteries opened up once again on the town to provide the would-be amphibians covering fire, the Confederates replied in kind. The engineers, having been subjected to such fire for hours, ran away from the boats and refused all assistance. It was now up to Baxter. Private Daniel McAdams of Company I of the 20th Massachusetts described what happened next:

> . . . the Cornel of the 7 Misagen Jumped in A Pontoon boat and asked his Men to Cross and Cornel Masey [Macy] and Capt Abbott tuck two others and asked the 20 Mass Boys to com over. They did Not hav to ask in Vain for We Ware all Willing to Go Whare Ever they led. So in the boats We Went and While 4 Got or Six Got the ors We stud over them With ower Rifles Reddy to Defend them.[20]

Lieutenant Ropes also remembered the moment when his regiment learned that they would be crossing the river in the face of the enemy fire:

> I was rather tired and almost asleep when Col. Hall rode up and said the 7th Michigan had volunteered to cross in pontoon boats. This was indeed a desperate thing, but a few moments some one said they were crossing, we heard sharp firing and some cheers, and then they were across and had occupied the nearest houses. We were ordered to fall in at the same time, and in a few moments marched down the bank and followed the 19th across in pontoon boats. . . .Some of the 7th Michigan were already being brought

back, among them the Lieut. Colonel [Henry Baxter] shot in the shoulder.[21]

The 7th Michigan successfully completed what would, in retrospect, comprise the first phase of the assault on Fredericksburg. Sixty to 70 Wolverines crossed in that first wave. Once across, they "formed under the bank and rushed upon the first street, [Water Street, now called Sophia Street] attacked the enemy, and, in the space of a few minutes, 31 prisoners were captured and a secure lodgement effected."[22] As the several dozen Midwesterners went about their business, Hall ordered the remaining Michiganders together with the 19th Massachusetts to attempt the crossing. Once they had crossed, he ordered the 7th Michigan to advance to the left of the landing point (estimated by the authors to be just to the right of where the finished bridgehead would eventually connect with the bank) and the 19th Massachusetts to deploy to the right.

Hall recalled that firing in the streets the town became "general and quite rapid." To his dismay, however, the engineers had not kept their promise to recommence work on the bridgehead once the crossings began. A direct order from Hall to the engineers to start work was refused with the excuse that General Woodbury was in command but he was not present to confirm the order. About this time, Hall observed what he believed was a brigade of the enemy advancing through the streets of the town in the direction of the river. At his request, Hunt's artillery opened in front of and on the flanks of the 7th Michigan and 19th Massachusetts. This fire, coupled with the newly-established Union presence on the opposite shore, temporarily did the trick. Hall stated that "All firing upon the bridge had been now silenced, and the bridge was rapidly completed."[23]

It was now time for the 20th Massachusetts to cross over the Rappahannock River. Sergeant John Summerhayes of Company I wrote to this cousin on Nantucket of what it felt like to cross the river in an open boat in the face of a deadly enemy, and how he drew strength from others around him:

Once only did I ever while under fire think there was any danger of losing my life by chance and that was when steering the old Pontoon boat across the Rappahonnnack, the boys lying in the bottom except three Rowers. While my body was wholly exposed the sharp shooters bullets knocked the splinters off the boat and oar, yet nary one touched me. [Lt. Leander F.] Alley was standing on the Gunwale of his boat cheering his men on. *What an example!* Could I, no matter how much of a Coward I might be, *flinch then?* Thou-

sands of men were cheering us on from the bank we had left—
'twas Glorious—'twas grand—bullets, shells and death were for-
gotton. Hurrah for victory and death to the Rebs—Grey backs were
at a discount.[24]

Private Murphey was in Lt. Alley's punt as it slipped across the dangerous
body of water:

> After getting into the boat two men sat down at the oars; one was
> Thomas Russell of this town [Nantucket], the other man I do not
> remember, but he pulled Russell right around and headed the boat
> upstream. Lieut. Leander F. Alley said to me, "Murphey, take that
> oar," which I did and we soon had the boat across on the other side
> where she grounded a few feet from the shore. We jumped out and
> waded to the land.[25]

Both Murphey and Summerhayes would have been astonished to learn that
Colonel Hall never intended the 20th Massachusetts to cross in boats. "An order
for the Twentieth Massachusetts Volunteers to move across the bridge the instant it was down," Hall remembered, "was incorrectly transmitted, so as to
cause Acting Major Macy, its commander, to throw it across in boats."[26] Intended or not, once the 20th Massachusetts was across, Hall ordered the regiment into line along the bank as a reserve to hold the shore should the
Confederates attempt to retake it. In the meantime, the 7th Michigan and 19th
Massachusetts had advanced into the buildings and backyards along Water
Street.

The fight for the streets of Fredericksburg was about to begin in earnest.

*   *   *

*My orders were to push forward the skirmishers and drive the
enemy from the city—bayonet every <u>male</u> found—<u>take</u> no prisoners.*

—Maj. George Nelson Macy to Col. William R. Lee.[27]

*The orders to the whole Brigade was to bayonet every armed man
found firing from a house, this being, I believe, contrary to the rules
of war, but was not of course obeyed.*

—Lt. Henry Ropes[28]

The streets of Fredericksburg form a near perfect grid along the banks of the Rappahannock. Running parallel with the river were the town's principal thoroughfares, set forth here in ascending order: Water Street, Main Street (also known as Caroline Street), Princess Anne Street and Charles Street. These main avenues are intersected at right angles by side streets that run from Water Street, and in that day eventually trailed off onto the eastern fringes of the plain preceding the stone wall at the foot of Marye's Heights. From north to south, those sides treets most closely associated with the street fight were Canal Street, Pitt Street, Hawke Street, Farquier Street, Lewis Street and Amelia Street.

After the portion of Water Street proximate to the Upper Bridge had been taken, the 19th Massachusetts deployed in the buildings and backyards to the right of Hawke Street while the 7th Michigan deployed similarly but to the left of Hawke. The river bank rose sharply to Water Street, which provided more than sufficient cover for the 20th Massachusetts still in line along the bank.[29]

With the Upper Bridge now completed, the 42nd New York, 59th New York and 127th Pennsylvania crossed over and augmented the gathering Federal force. At the same time, Colonel Hall ordered the 20th Massachusetts to form in column of companies on Water Street. The Bay Staters passed Hawke Street on their right as they marched towards the bridge, but the column was fired upon as it passed the next street, Farquier, and the citizen guide leading the regiment was killed.[30]

As casualties mounted, Colonel Hall felt pressed by his own troops pouring over the bridge as well as by the gathering darkness:

> Upon attempting to cross the second street, it became evident that the enemy was in considerable force, and could only be dislodged by desperate fighting. It was fast growing dark, the troops were being crowded near the bridge head in a compact and unmanageable mass, and I was informed that the whole division was to cross to hold the city. It was impracticable, in my opinion, to relieve the press by throwing troops into the streets, where they could only be shot down, unable to return the fire. To give time to fight the enemy in his own way, I sent urgent requests to the rear to have the column halted on the other side of the river, but was ordered to push ahead.[31]

"To fight the enemy in his own way," may well help explain the order to bayonet any prisoners, probably given by Hall, the senior commander on the scene. What mattered most at that moment, however, was one order Hall issued that the officers and men of the 20th Massachusetts were prepared to obey without question. "I ordered Acting Major Macy," Hall said, "to clear the street leading from the bridge at all hazards."[32] Sergeant Albert B. Holmes of Company I remembered:

> We formed in column by Co and marched up towards Caroline street a piece. The Rebs opened on us from windows and doors and from behind the houses. We had no choice and after loosing half of our Co we made a rush for the Houses[,] broke in doors and chased the Rebs out the back yards returning shot for shot and finally drove them from the town. The victory was ours but the cost was great. We buried fifteen of my company in one yard on the corner of Caroline street. . .[33]

The 20th Massachusetts, personally led by George Nelson Macy, turned right on to Farquier Street. Company I, comprised largely of Nantucket and Martha's Vineyard boys, was in the van and led by Henry Livermore Abbott, whose *sang-froid* was fast becoming legend. Abbott would later command the regiment and fall in battle in 1864. Behind Company I was Company K (which included Lt. Henry Ropes), with Company A bringing up the rear. The men were shoulder-to-shoulder four abreast, and the column crowded to the right side of the street. As such, they were easy targets for Confederate marksmen concealed in the buildings along the street. Not that much marksmanship was required. In some cases, enemy snipers were only a few feet from their victims.

Murderous Confederate fire was not the only impediment confronting the 20th Massachusetts. Its supports, according to Major Macy, acted with great timidity:

> I led forth immediately upon rising above the bank we were under a hot fire from houses and fences from all directions. My guide faltered—I pushed him forward and he dropped dead—shot. Abbott's Company [Company I] was 60 strong—I immediately ordered him to form by platoons and open fire—we still moved forward. The skirmishers I came upon—they had halted in rear of the houses on Caroline St. I could not get them to move farther, the fire was dreadful. I sent rear for orders and was ordered 'push forward'— drive them out. "Forward 20th in column"—I used some strong language to the officers in command of pickets—ending by referring them to a very hot place, but they would not move forward— drive them out.[34]

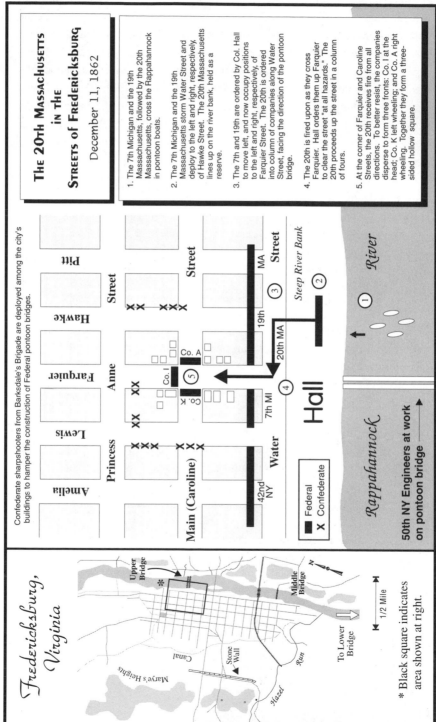

THE 20TH MASSACHUSETTS IN THE STREETS OF FREDERICKSBURG

December 11, 1862

Mark A. Moore

1. The 7th Michigan and the 19th Massachusetts, followed by the 20th Massachusetts, cross the Rappahannock in pontoon boats.

2. The 7th Michigan and the 19th Massachusetts storm Water Street and deploy to the left and right, respectively, of Hawke Street. The 20th Massachusetts lines up on the river bank, held as a reserve.

3. The 7th and 19th are ordered by Col. Hall to move left, and now occupy positions to the left and right, respectively, of Farquier Street. The 20th is ordered into column of companies along Water Street, facing the direction of the pontoon bridge.

4. The 20th is fired upon as they cross Farquier. Hall orders them up Farquier to clear the street "at all hazards." The 20th proceeds up the street in a column of fours.

5. At the corner of Farquier and Caroline Streets, the 20th receives fire from all directions. To better resist, the companies disperse to form three fronts: Co. I at the head; Co. K left wheeling; and Co. A right wheeling. Together they form a three-sided hollow square.

Confederate sharpshooters from Barksdale's Brigade are deployed among the city's buildings to hamper the construction of Federal pontoon bridges.

Pitt Street

Hawke Street

Farquier

Anne

Lewis

Princess

Amelia

Main (Caroline)

Water Street

Co. A

Co. I

Co. K

7th MI

42nd NY

19th MA

20th MA

Hall

Steep River Bank

Rappahannock River

Federal
X Confederate

50th NY Engineers at work on pontoon bridge →

Frederichsburg, Virginia

Upper Bridge

Middle Bridge

To Lower Bridge

Canal

Stone Wall

Mary's Heights

Hazel Run

N

1/2 Mile

* Black square indicates area shown at right.

The original plan was for the 7th Michigan to advance ahead of the 20th Massachusetts as skirmishers. Deterred by enemy fire, however, many of the Michiganders took cover in an alley between two buildings on Farquier Street just up the corner from Water Street. Similarly, the 19th Massachusetts had been deployed in the buildings and yards on the right side of Farquier Street and, like the 7th Michigan, did not advance in conjunction with the 20th. The 42nd New York was on the extreme left of the 7th Michigan around the buildings and backyards lining the foot of Lewis Street and Amelia Street. Thus, out of four regiments, only one—the 20th Massachusetts—moved out and attempted to clear the enemy from the buildings of Fredericksburg.

Lieutenant Ropes gave additional details of the fighting in a letter written soon after the battle:

> The 20th advanced up the street, and when the head of the column got where the 7th Michigan men were, on the left, in a kind of alley way, and occupying a house, Macy called to them to go ahead. Capt. Hunt, their commanding officer was there, and he hesitated and refused. Macy was obliged to halt and urge him to go forward. Capt. Hunt still refused, saying he had no orders, and Macy, much irritated, told him his orders, which were very plain, to go forward and follow the 7th. Orders came from the rear to press on, Hunt still hung back, saying the Rebels were there in force, and "no man could live around that corner". . . .Macy was of course terribly angry, and turned off saying: "Go to hell with your Regiment then."[35]

Ropes reported that the failure of the 7th Michigan to advance stalled the 20th Massachusetts' progress up Farquier Street some "2 or 3 minutes," after which the column advanced towards Caroline Street. Casualties were substantial and growing, a desperate situation recollected by Private Murphey:

> . . .our men began dropping at every point, those struck in the vital parts dropping without a sound, but those wounded otherwise would cry out with pain as they fell or limped to the rear. . . .Where men fell and left a vacant place other men stepped into their places and although death stared us in the face there was not a man who faltered. Our chief company officer Capt. H. L. Abbott said "hold your fire boys, until you see something to fire at."[36]

Lieutenant Ropes wrote that when the regiment arrived at the corner of Farquier and Caroline Street and attempted to advance through the intersection, "a tremendous and deadly fire swept down our front and left. . . .It staggered the Column," he stated, "but in a moment they pressed on, led by Abbott in his usual fearless manner."[37]

For Private Murphey, that particular intersection was destined to be one he would remember for the rest of his life. "We had now arrived at the corner of a cross street called Caroline street," he recalled, "and I, being on the left flank of the company, turned to look down the street to see if anything could be seen to fire at and bringing my gun to the ready at the same time." Murphey did not have time to find a target. "At that moment I felt a sharp stinging pain on the right side of my face," he explained, "and presto, I knew no more." Murphey had been shot in the face. He would recover, but for him the Battle of Fredericksburg was over.[38]

Murphey's reaction to his wounding and detailed description somehow seems typical of a time when acceptance of hardship was more commonplace:

> When I came to I was lying on the ground where I had fallen, and the company had advanced a short distance up the street. The balls were still flying thick around me and I realized I was wounded. I clapped my hand to my face to stop the flow of blood but it was no use. It flowed between my fingers and down into my clothing and filled me full. I got up rather faint, and a feeling of madness came over me, and a word in your ear gentle reader and let it go no further, I swore; I cursed the whole southern confederacy from Virginia to the gulf of Mexico; but on second thought I realized it was war and banished such thoughts from my mind and made my way across the river to the a hospital called the Lacy House. . .[39]

Private McAdams would also have special reason to remember that intersection and in particular Murphey's wounding:

> When We Got to the Cross Streets We had to form A Hollow Square for We Were Receiving thair fire from all Quarters but We Kept Wright on. About this time A young fellow by the Name of Murphy [Murphey] got struck in the face and it Glanced and Hit Me in the Brest and Knocked me abot ten yards down the Street. Lieut Ally Got Ahold of Me and asked if I Was Hurt. I felt in My Brest and Could Not find any Blood. I told him I Would go in Agane.[40]

The sweeping enemy fire encountered at the corner of Caroline and Farquier Streets may have had its origins in a circumstance that adds weight to more romantic notions of the Civil War. Towards night, Confederate Maj. Gen. Lafayette McLaws, whose division included William Barksdale's redoubtable Mississippians and Floridians, witnessed the progress of Union arms advancing into the town and ordered Barksdale's men to withdraw. The 21st Mississippi, which had been engaged near the Middle Bridge, was ordered to cover the withdrawal of those troops facing the insurgent Federals.

The rear detachment of the 21st Mississippi, that which faced the 20th Massachusetts, was commanded by Lt. Lane Brandon, a former Harvard classmate of Henry L. Abbott. Brandon learned from Massachusetts prisoners that it was Abbott's company in the Union van. As Douglas Southall Freeman tells the tale:

> That was enough for Brandon. Cost what it might, he would whip Abbott then and there! Brandon halted his rearguard, turned about, attacked the Twentieth Massachusetts and momentarily pressed it back. He was preparing to carry the contest back through the town, if he could, when his delay in closing the rear was discovered. Orders the most peremptory were sent to him to break off the fight. So mad was he, even then, to outdo his friend Abbott that he had to be put under arrest.[41]

At this time, the 20th Massachusetts' column was ordered to divide by companies to better resist what seemed like enemy fire coming from all quarters. Company I passed through the intersection of Caroline Street and continued up Farquier Street, while Company K executed a left wheel at the intersection to face the southern stretch of Caroline Street. Company A simultaneously wheeled to the right and formed a line across the northern stretch of Caroline Street. This movement is probably the basis for the hollow square formation recalled by Private McAdams.

Major Macy wrote of the horror of the routinely overlooked street fighting at Fredericksburg, and the lonely isolation suffered by his regiment as members of his unit were "murdered" in the thoroughfares of one of the country's most historic cities:

> Here we cleared the houses near us, but shot came from far and near—we could see no one and were simply murdered—as every shot of the enemy took effect. How I escaped I cannot say, as I was

everywhere and more than a dozen actually fell upon me. I trembled for Abbott—he did nobly. Here we fought for 2 1/2 hours, and night came to our relief. We silenced the flank fire—Abbott advanced about 30 yards, but it was no use, as we were the only ones fighting and no one supporting the right or left—because the troops sent there <u>would not</u> advance.[42]

What Major Macy did in response to the 20th Massachusetts' lethal isolation was recalled by Lieutenant Ropes, who was now commanding a mere remnant of Company K: "The men were Killed and wounded so fast that the rest of the Regiment was immediately called up and supported the Companies first in position," he reported. In this manner, "Companies D, G amd C came up and filled that part of the street my Company could not cover. The entire place was heaped with bodies," he continued, "our guns were getting clogged, our fire slack, and Macy sent back urgent requests for help and for the Regiments on our right and left to advance. . ."[43]

The situation at the intersection had become desperate. A few yards up Farquier, Rebel soldiers took positions in "a small house on the left of Company I from which Abbott vainly tried to dislodge them by entering a house on his left." Company A, facing the right branch of Caroline Street, had found the fire too severe and had taken cover in nearby houses. Company K held its ground, but at a terrible price. By the time it was belatedly relieved by the 59th New York, Lieutenant Ropes could rally only eight men.

*   *   *

"Yes your Regt. is more like old times" (meaning thereby the old Regular Army where Officers were Gentlemen) "than anything I have seen in the Army." wh. in connection with other remarks about the perfection of their present condition and their behavior in the Field rather pleased me—[Colonel Norman J. Hall] said "The 20th have no poetry in a fight" and there is about as little excitement & hullabulloo on those occasions as may be—At Fsburg Macy says quietly "Mr. Abbott you will take your first platoon forward" to wh. A. "1st Platoon forward—March" and walks quietly ahead—His 1st Platoon is knocked to pieces (He lost that day 30 out of 60—10 shot dead) instantly—"You'll have to put in the 2nd" says Col. H. "2nd Platoon forward" and A. leads them too into the storm with the same semi indifferent air that he has when

drilling a Battn. I really very much doubt whether there is any Regt.
wh. can compare with ours in the Army of the Potomac.

—Oliver Wendell Holmes, Jr., Captain, Company A,
20th Massachusetts Volunteer Infantry.[44]

Nightfall and the gradual withdrawal of Confederate forces finally ended the bloody affair in the streets of Fredericksburg. It was reported that afterwards, Abbott led what remained of his drained command to the riverbank for the evening. The 20th Massachusetts had started the day with 335 men. Of these, 113 were killed or wounded, a 33% casualty rate; yet, the "ball" on the rising plain before Marye's Heights was not set to open for two more days.[45]

In certain respects, the river crossing and street fight were microcosms of the larger Fredericksburg story: poor Federal tactical planning, dogged Confederate resistance, and a bottom-up valor exemplified by common soldiers and their immediate officers. Certainly Civil War tactics, deficient in so many respects, completely failed to prepare the "20 Mass Boys" for the house-to-house combat they experienced. The massed fire expected from the shoulder-to-shoulder column of companies, wheels and lines of battle was utterly useless against a largely dispersed and concealed enemy. As the casualty figures suggest and as common sense would imply, massed formations in narrow streets provide easy fodder for an ambitious and well-armed enemy.

As the widespread cheers that rang in Sergeant Summerhayes' ears would indicate, the sight of the 7th Michigan, 19th Massachusetts and 20th Massachusetts rowing across the river was in plain view of much of the Federal army. So, too, was the awful street fight and the terrible casualties inflicted by the sharpshooters and building-dwellers dressed in gray. During the early phase of the Civil War, sharpshooting was viewed as unmanly, in some quarters a form of cowardice whose results were regarded as little more than murder.[46] Perhaps the sight of the slaughter in the town contributed in some measure to the anger of the Northern troops encamped in Fredericksburg on the evening of December 11th, for it was sacked completely by the morning of the 12th.

Perhaps because the river crossing and street fight were witnessed by so many, the accomplishments of the 7th Michigan and the 19th and 20th Massachusetts were celebrated not just in the army, but in the press and among poets as well. George Henry Boker, a poet and dramatist (and later United States Minister to Russia and Turkey) wrote the poem "The Crossing at Frederickburg," inspired in part by an interview with a certain young captain of the 20th

Massachusetts who was destined to be an associate justice of the United States Supreme Court:

> They leaped into the rocking shallops,
> Ten offered where one could go,
> The breeze was alive with laughter
> Till the boatman began to row.
>
> "How many? I judge four hundred;"
> "Who are they? I know to a man;"
> Our own Nineteenth and Twentieth,
> And the Seventh Michigan.
>
> Then the shore where the rebels harbored,
> Was fringed with a gush of flame,
> And buzzing like bees o'er water
> The swarms of their bullets came.
>
> And many a brave stout fellow,
> Who sprang in the boats with mirth,
> Ere they made that fatal crossing
> Was a load of lifeless earth.
>
> And many a brave stout fellow,
> Whose limbs with strength were rife,
> Was torn and crushed and shattered—
> A helpless wreck for life.
>
> Cheer after cheer we sent them,
> As only armies can,
> Cheer for old Massachusetts!
> Cheers for young Michigan![47]

Endnotes:

1. Richard F. Miller and Robert F. Mooney, *The Civil War: The Nantucket Experience* (Nantucket, 1994), pp. 83-84. The 20th Massachusetts was organized in Readville,

MA in late August and early September 1861. With the exception of the men enlisted in Nantucket by Lieutenant George Macy, no particular locality was represented in the regiment. In this respect the 20th MA probably differed from every other Massachusetts regiment, and more nearly resembled those of the Regular Army. While most of Company I hailed from Nantucket, Martha's Vineyard, and Cape Cod, the balance came from the state's eastern counties, many from in and around Boston.

After participating in the fiasco at Ball's Bluff later that year (where the regiment lost 38 men killed and mortally wounded), the Bay Staters performed good service on the Virginia peninsula in the Seven Days Battles (Savage's Station, Glendale, and Malvern Hill) and in the Maryland Campaign at the Battle of Antietam. After the fighting in the battles in and around Fredericksburg from December 11-13, 1862, which is the subject of this article, the 20th went on to see heavy action at Gettysburg (44 killed and mortally wounded), the Wilderness (36 killed and mortally wounded), Spotsylvania (20 killed and mortally wounded), Cold Harbor (12 killed and mortally wounded), and Petersburg (12 killed and mortally wounded). Of those that served in the 20th during the war, some 260 were killed, over 13% of its members. William F. Fox, *Regimental Losses in the American Civil War, 1861-1865* (Dayton, 1985), p. 164; Frederick H. Dyer, *A Compendium of the War of the Rebellion* (Dayton, 1978), pp. 1254-1255. For more information on the full service of the 20th Massachusetts Infantry, with special attention to the sentiments of its Harvard officers corps, see "The Copperhead Regiment: The 20th Massachusetts Infantry," by Anthony J. Milano, *Civil War Regiments*, Vol. 3, No. 1 (1993), pp. 31-63.

2. Ibid., p. 83.

3. Winfield Scott Hancock Papers, U.S. Army Military History Institute, Carlisle Barracks, PA, Major Geo. N. Macy, 20th Massachusetts Infantry Diary Letter: Fredericksburg, hereinafter cited as the Macy Letter. On December 2, 1862, Captain Macy was promoted to acting major and took over command of the regiment, replacing Col. William R. Lee, who was absent due to illness. Macy's promotion to major was made permanent on December 18, 1862. The authors wish to thank William D. Matter of Harrisburg, Pennsylvania for bringing this letter to their attention.

4. Vorin E. Whan, Jr., *Fiasco At Fredericksburg,* (Gaithersburg, ———), p. 37.

5. Macy Letter.

6. Henry Ropes to John Codman Ropes, Dec. 18, 1862, Henry Ropes Letters, Boston Public Library, hereinafter cited as the Ropes Letter. Excerpts therefrom are published courtesy of the Trustees of the Boston Public Library.

7. U.S. War Department, *The War of the Rebellion: The Official Records of the Union and Confederate Armies*, 128 vols. (Washington, DC, 1890-1901), Series I, Vol. 21, p. 175, hereinafter cited as *OR.* All references are to series I.

8. Ropes Letter.

9. Macy Letter.

10. *OR* 21, p. 174.

11. Ibid., p. 191.

12. Ibid.

13. Ibid., p. 578.

14. Ibid., p. 183.

15. Ibid., p. 171.

16. Ropes Letter.

17. "A Short History of the Service of Daniel McAdams in Company I 20 Regiment Mass Vol., 30 years after the War Wrote from Memory," MOLLUS Collection, Houghton Library, Harvard University, Cambridge, MA., quoted courtesy of the Houghton Library, and hereinafter cited as McAdams, "A Short History." The authors wish to thank Leslie Morris, Curator of Rare Manuscripts for the Houghton for her generous assistance.

18. *OR* 21, p. 183.

19. This account has been taken from Edward G. Longacre, *The Man Behind the Guns* (Cranbury, 1977) pp. 132-133.

20. McAdams, "A Short History."

21. Ropes Letter.

22. *OR* 21, p. 283.

23. Ibid.

24. John W. Summerhayes, "Letters of a Soldier," *Massachusetts Magazine*, n.d.

25. Miller and Mooney, *Nantucket Experience*, p. 87.

26. *OR* 21, p. 283.

27. Macy Letter.

28. Ropes Letter.

29. The authors wish to thank Robert K. Krick for producing a map indicating the original street names of Fredericksburg at the time of the battle, and the positions of Union and Confederate units.

30. There is some dispute as to whether the 20th Massachusetts battled its way up Farquier, or on the preceding street, Hawke. Based on firsthand accounts as well as other evidence, the authors are persuaded that Farquier Street hosted the fight—and the Bay Staters.

31. *OR* 21, p. 283.

32. Ibid.

33. Account of Albert B. Holmes, October 17, 1896, MOLLUS Collection, Houghton Library, Harvard University, Cambridge, Massachusetts, quoted courtesy of the Houghton Library.

34. Macy Letter.

35. Ropes Letter.

36. Miller and Mooney, *Nantucket Experience*, pp. 87-88.

37. Ropes Letter.

38. Miller and Mooney, *Nantucket Experience*, p. 88.

39. Ibid.

40. McAdams, "A Short History."

41. Douglas Southall Freeman, *Lee's Lieutenants: A Study in Command*, 3 vols. (New York, 1943), vol. 2, p. 338.

42. Macy Letter.

43. Ropes Letter.

44. Oliver Wendell Holmes, Jr., *Touched With Fire: Civil War Letters and Diary of Oliver Wendell Holmes, Jr.*, edited by Mark DeWolfe Howe, (Cambridge, 1946), p. 90.

45. Henry Livermore Abbott, *Fallen Leaves: The Civil War Letters of Major Henry Livermore Abbott*, edited by Robert Garth Scott, (Kent, Ohio, 1991), p. 17. Colonel Hall's brigade, including the 20th Massachusetts, participated in the battle on the 13th of December. In the advance against Maj. Gen. James Longstreet's First Corps, during which the brigade suffered under a "heavy and well-aimed fire of infantry in the front, and a terrible one of artillery against the right flank," Col. Hall proudly reported in his after-action report that "The Twentieth Massachusetts stood firm and returned the fire of the enemy. . . ." *OR* 21, p. 284.

46. Gerald F. Linderman, *Embattled Courage* (New York, 1989), pp. 147-148.

47. Miller and Mooney, *Nantucket Experience*, pp. 85-86.

The Preservation Report

Like most Civil War battlefields, especially those in northern Virginia, Fredericksburg has changed significantly since the battles of December 1862. While it is not the purpose (nor is there sufficient space) in this brief essay to set forth and describe all of these changes, there are some special sites of interest to readers of this collection of essays that are worthy of mention.

The 20th Massachusetts Infantry: Two of the three river crossing sites are currently accessible to the public. The middle pontoon crossing spanned from what is now a Stafford County park at Ferry Farm—boyhood home of George Washington—to the city dock, at the southern end of Sophia Street. Today the city dock is a public boat launch. The Fredericksburg side of the upper pontoon crossing is owned by the National Park Service and contains historical markers. The park currently offers a pair of new brochures interpreting important sites on a trail linking the river crossing and city fighting to the Sunken Road. Many of the Civil War-era buildings that witnessed the street fighting so well described in Richard Miller's article still stand today. Some of them are identified with Historic Fredericksburg Foundation, Inc. markers, indicating the date of construction and often the name of the original owners. A leisurely stroll from the river crossings through the streets of Fredericksburg, armed with the excellent map accompanying Miller's essay (drafted by cartographer Mark Moore) will substantially enhance one's understanding of this important but little-known engagement.

The Irish Brigade and *The Death of General Cobb*: Although the open plain in front of the Sunken Road (crossed by Private William McCarter and defended by Cobb's Georgians) was about one-half mile wide during the battle, the park has until recently had only a narrow strip of land one block wide, with the remainder of the field comprising a residential area. The park boundary was recently expanded to allow for a full block of park property in front of the Confederate line, that is, between the Sunken Road and what is now Willis Street (one block to the east). With the limited amount of money earmarked for the acquisition of land, some of the homes have been purchased by the park, and to date a gasoline station and one house have been razed.

The only section of Marye's Heights within the park is the southern end of the ridge, which became the National Cemetery shortly after the war ended. The Marye family home, Brompton, still stands, and is visible from within the park when standing at the northern end of the Stone Wall. The home is owned by the Commonwealth of Virginia and is the residence for the president of Mary Washington College.

The Pennsylvania Reserves and *Jackson's Artillery*: Linking the Sunken Road sector of the battlefield with the Prospect Hill area is a four mile road called Lee Drive, which essentially follows the original Confederate battle line. The park was established along what is termed the "Antietam Plan," which means that the original design was intended only to procure small tracts of land along routes providing access to the key areas of fighting, as well as acquiring earthworks and other physical remains. It was *not* designed to procure large tracts of the battlefield itself. In most cases in which the Antietam Plan was employed, it was felt that the land use would not substantially change, and therefore access to views of the battlefield were desired rather than the areas of intense conflict themselves. The portion of the Fredericksburg battlefield actually within the park, as found on a park service brochure or map, therefore, does not indicate the ground where the heaviest fighting occurred. The sections of the park along the four miles of Confederate battle line between the two areas of severe fighting are often wider and better protected than the portions of the line that were actually under attack.

While Prospect Hill and the various artillery emplacements thereon are preserved, they are not visited nearly as often as the more famous Sunken Road/Stone Wall sector of the field. Davidson's artillery position, at Bernard Cabins, was recently added to the park. A trail had been constructed to eventually guide visitors to the site, and as soon as markers are completed and erected, this important ground will be accessible and interpreted.

Both the knoll upon which Major Latimer's pieces were posted and Brockenbrough's artillery position are just outside of the park's boundary; they remain essentially unaltered from their original state. Likewise, the Confederate artillery and cavalry position south of Hamilton's Crossing is also outside of the park. The Union artillery positions, the Union staging area, and the scene of John Pelham's stand early in the battle are all well to the east of the park. Along the Richmond Stage Road are two sets of historical markers indicating the Pelham site and the start of the Federal attack.

Book Reviews

The Shipwreck of Their Hopes: The Battles for Chattanooga, by Peter Cozzens (University of Illinois Press, 1325 South Oak Street, Champaign, IL 61820), 1994. Photos, maps, illus., biblio., index. d.j., 515pp. Cloth. $29.95

Peter Cozzens is a foreign service official with the United States Department of State who has written three books on Civil War history, all of them dealing with military events in Tennessee and Georgia. In addition to this book, he also authored *This Terrible Sound: The Battle of Chickamauga,* and *No Better Place to Die: The Battle of Stones River.*

Cozzens' narrative on Chattanooga begins with the promotion of U. S. Grant as commander of the Military Division of the Mississippi, his meeting in Louisville, Kentucky, with Edwin M. Stanton, and his removal of William S. Rosecrans as commander of the Army of the Cumberland. Other early chapters contain detailed topographical descriptions of the Chattanooga area and include a number of maps. Readers should pay close attention to this information because it makes the later narrative much easier to follow. Cozzens then launches into a description of the Union assault on Brown's Ferry and the opening of the so-called "Cracker Line" to relieve the starving Federal troops in the city. Next he describes in utmost detail the battles for Lookout Mountain and Missionary Ridge. From the preliminary movements of troops on both sides to the final defeat of Confederate forces, Cozzens devotes about 100 pages to each battle.

This book may shatter some historical conceptions of both Union and Confederate military leaders, for Cozzens is quick to criticize where he finds fault. On the one hand, he regards William T. Sherman as a timid commander, prone to make mistakes. What helped elevate Sherman's historical reputation, claims Cozzens, was Grant's support and willingness to overlook the general's faults. On the other hand, Cozzens feels sympathy for George H. Thomas and writes that Grant's dislike of Thomas caused him to ignore the general's ability. Indeed, Grant took full credit for the bravery of Thomas' troops in their legendary charge up the center of Missionary Ridge by overlooking the fact that he originally ordered them merely to take Confederate trenches at the bottom of the slope. Cozzens' hero on the Union side is Philip Sheridan. Previously a division commander in the Army of the Cumberland, Sheridan earned Cozzens' praise and Grant's attention when he continued to pursue Confederate troops down the eastern slope of Missionary Ridge after most Union commanders were content with driving the Southerners off the heights overlooking Chattanooga.

Cozzens has his champions on the Confederate side as well. Like Steven Woodworth in *Jefferson Davis and His Generals: The Failure of Confederate Command in the West*, Cozzens paints a much more favorable picture of Braxton Bragg than most historians. He admits that Bragg made errors but still contends that it was overwhelming force, not the failure of command, that caused the Confederate defeat. James Longstreet, however, comes in for special disapproval. His open criticism of Bragg's ability and his unwillingness to follow orders or take Union moves seriously bordered, in Cozzens' opinion, on insubordination.

The book is written adequately except for Cozzens' occasional use of slang phrases, such as certain generals needing "a kick in the pants." He also tends to lapse into digressions that add little to the story—see pages 114 and 115 on the death of Sherman's son, for example. The most impressive aspect of the book is its depth of research, though several recent works are missing. Despite Cozzens' concentration on portions of Sherman's personal life, John Marszalek's biography of the general apparently was not consulted. Still, the list of manuscript and contemporary sources consulted covers almost eight printed pages.

The major drawback of the book is Cozzens' failure to distinguish the important from the unimportant. Readers may find themselves bogged down in detail and have difficulty following the major thread of the narrative. Constant citing of the exact minute when troops began to move or when messages were sent and arrived seems in many instances to have no importance to the overall outcome of the battle and makes for tedious reading. Similarly, Cozzens' tendency to give the author of every quotation, no matter how minor, overwhelms the reader with unimportant detail. On page 169, for example, Cozzens mentions six different officers in a brief, six-line paragraph.

The book is also marred by its lack of interpretation. Except for evaluating the roles of various commanders, Cozzens ignores the overall significance of the battles for Chattanooga. The closest he comes to analyzing their importance occurs on page 391, when he notes that the campaign cemented the relationship between Grant, Sherman, and Sheridan. Surely the loss of Chattanooga for the Confederacy and the Union's ability to capture a city that had been one of its major objectives for over two years must have had greater significance than creating stronger ties of comradeship among three men.

Readers who thrive on narrative covering military events will find the book worthwhile; those who do not may come away disappointed.

Eugene H. Berwanger   Colorado State University

The Fredericksburg Campaign: Decision on the Rappahannock, by Gary Gallagher (The University of North Carolina Press, P.O. Box 228, Chapel Hill, NC 27515-2288), 1995. Photos, illus., maps, bibliographic essay, index. 243pp. Cloth. $24.95.

What is the one quotation everyone remembers about the Fredericksburg Campaign? Of course, Robert E. Lee's memorable, if cryptic, "It is well that war is so terrible—we should grow too fond of it!" Well, not exactly, as we discover in this splendid collection of essays on the 1862 campaign; Lee perhaps said it a little differently. Of course, the point is that in this offering, edited by Gary Gallagher, we look at this well-known military campaign anew and find that a little plowing makes for a fertile field of inquiry.

Today, a student of the Civil War could travel to Fredericksburg, Virginia, arise early one morning, and in one whirlwind day visit the sites of four major engagements of the war: Fredericksburg, 1862; Chancellorsville, 1863; and the Wilderness and Spotsylvania Court House, 1864, all located just a few miles from one another. The Fredericksburg Campaign of November and December of 1862 has long been looked upon as the epitome of the incompetence of military leadership of the Army of the Potomac. In the midst of a month of gloom, President Lincoln despaired for the Union cause the week after the battle: "It appears to me the Almighty is against us, and I can hardly see a ray of hope."

An authoritative modern treatment of the battle, as has characterized a number of the war's major campaigns, has not yet been written. The modern works available are either along the lines of introduction to the battle, or focus solely upon select military aspects. But until that detailed account appears, the present work is the best single volume to have on your shelf on this topic. *The Fredericksburg Campaign* contains seven essays by Civil War scholars and authors and a useful bibliographic essay by the editor.

Two of the most unique and interesting essays deal with the physical impact of the battle upon Confederate civilians, and how Southerners viewed the battle in its aftermath. William Blair examines a topic often neglected: the impact of the battle upon the citizens who lived in Fredericksburg. This intriguing offering studies the resiliency of the people of Frederickburg in the presence of enemy occupation in an active war zone. The disruption of lives is seen also in the context of the slave population of the vicinity, and concludes with speculation on whether or not morale in the vicinity waned or strengthened with the ordeal.

Gary Gallagher's essay explores the complex response to the battle by the Southern populace as well as by the men of Lee's army. It seems to be the general assumption today that Southern civilians praised such a clear-cut Union defeat, while we simultaneously take Douglas Southall Freeman's lead by noting the despondency of Confederate officers, particularly Lee, who regretted the escape of the Army of the Potomac from destruction. Gallagher's essay, based upon the statements of 135 individuals across the Confederacy, sifts through the nuances of the Confederate response, leading to a rich discussion of the political/morale impact of the campaign. Gallagher concludes with an insightful look at Lee's odd view of the battle, and the perspective of viewing battles in the context of waging successful war.

As one would expect, two of the essays examine Union and Confederate military leadership during the campaign. William Marvel, biographer of Ambrose E. Burnside, examines the Union high command. His analysis examines interpretations of other historians of the campaign, as well as the grand tactics planned by Burnside and how they were carried out by his subordinates. We are also treated to fascinating insights of Burnside's relations with his corps commanders. In the end, however, if Marvel's attempt to resuscitate Burnside's dismal military reputation does not quite win us over, we will at least come away believing the blame should be spread more evenly.

The only weak link in this volume is the essay provided by Alan T. Nolan on Confederate leadership at Fredericksburg. Nolan's contribution provides us with a useful chronological treatment of Lee's movement of Longstreet's and Jackson's corps to Fredericksburg, rather than to the North Anna position which Lee preferred. The unusual situation on the Confederate right flank, about which controversy has swirled concerning the gap in Jackson's line, is given only a cursory treatment. As far as how the Army of Northern Virginia personnel perceived the significance of the battle, it should suffice to compare Nolan's sparse observations with those of Gary Gallagher's essay.

Two essays explore in depth a theme which strikes anyone who spends time studying this battle, the factors that make the very name "Fredericksburg" a byword for the horrors and carnage of war. George C. Rable describes vividly what it was like to be in the ranks in such a maelstrom of shot and shell, from the heart rending description of the attack of Meagher's Irish Brigade, to the sights and sounds of field hospitals and burial details. Rable's article culminates with an examination of how such a Federal disaster tested the faith and will of the United States government and populace. Carol Reardon's essay, a model of its kind, details the assault of Humphreys' Pennsylvania Division. One wishes that space could have permitted Reardon to treat the attack of the Second Corps, the assault that preceded Humphreys' advance, but in dramatic fashion we glean a sense of what happened to the Second Corps as the survivors obstructed the advance of Humphrey's two brigades and cried out to Humphrey's men that they would be slaughtered. The splendid detail of this impressive essay ends with the postwar skirmishes of Union veterans, as men of the Second Corps and Fifth Corps vied for attention for what they had done at Fredericksburg.

Finally, we end up in the mud with Burnside, as A. Wilson Greene takes us through the travails of the Army of the Potomac in the six weeks after Fredericksburg, to the dismissal of Burnside in January 1863. Greene provides an excellent account of the dismal Union fiasco known popularly as the "Mud March." Attention is also given to the process which led Lincoln to select Joe Hooker to succeed Burnside. And I cannot help but like any writing which uses such an expressive phrase as this one, when Wilson describes Burnside's leadership in the weeks following the Battle of Fredericksburg: "Burnside would sink or swim on his own, paddling about in the shark tank on the Rappahannock" (p. 216).

For anyone who thinks highly of the recently published essays on the Gettysburg Campaign, also edited by Gary Gallagher, you will not be disappointed by this volume on Fredericksburg. The new perspectives contained in this volume are almost all fresh and provocative and based upon admirable scholarship. No study of the war in the Eastern Theater will be complete without this volume.

David P. Smith   Dallas, Texas

Marching to Cold Harbor: Victory & Failure, 1864, by R. Wayne Maney (White Mane Publishing Co., Inc., P.O. Box 152, Shippensburg, PA 17257), 1994. Photos., appendix, notes, biblio., index. 270pp. Cloth. $29.95.

In an intensive and highly detailed manner, Maney has dealt with the military movements of the Army of the Potomac commanded by Lt. Gen. Ulysses S. Grant, and the Army of Northern Virginia, commanded by Gen. Robert E. Lee, from May 4 through June 12, 1864. He assiduously combed over 800 manuscripts, books, newspapers, and periodicals, including many eyewitness, primarysource accounts from the Wilderness to Spotsylvania; to Haw's Shop to Bethesada Church; and finally, to the second battle of Cold Harbor.

Historians often give short shrift to the Civil War after the surrender of Vicksburg and the Confederate defeat at Gettysburg in 1863. By remaining active in the field, Confederate armies could, at best, hope that anti-war Democrats, northern Copperheads, and peace-minded Republicans would force a negotiated peace by President Abraham Lincoln; that some European nation desperate for Southern cotton would intervene miraculously on the side of the

Confederacy; or that England, France, or Russia (or all three) would serve as brokers for mediation between the disaffected sections.

For any Civil War historian desiring a fully-documented account of the movements of both armies to Cold Harbor, with appropriate block quotations cited from primary sources, one need look no further. However, if the reader is seeking a broader perspective in the interpretation of this campaign rather than a detailed, focused narrative, he will experience a sense of frustration. While Maney provides a factual portrait appropriately supported by primary documentation, sometimes the pace of his narrative is broken by his excessive, lengthy use of these quotes. Simply put, strings of block quotes over several pages are distracting to the reader.

Maney's research efforts, especially in finding often obscure published primary documentation, are to be admired. He misses the mark, however, by not placing this crucial campaign in the larger perspective of evolving warfare. It had become clear by 1864 that outdated tactics had not kept up with new weapons and technology. Indeed, the evolution of defensive trench warfare—complete with a parapet and *abatis* in front and entrenched batteries in the rear—as employed by both Union and Confederate armies over the last year of the War would have to be rediscovered in Europe during World War I. Unfortunately, Maney makes little effort to place the events of the spring of 1864 in a broader perspective, and this is the monograph's greatest weakness. Both Grant and Lee should be credited for recognizing that new strategies of war had evolved, and, in spite of the criticism—especially of Grant's apparent cavalier waste of manpower—that those tactics which may have been appropriate in 1861 were clearly no longer appropriate in 1864.

Another weakness becomes apparent when evaluating the monograph's footnotes. There is an inordinate amount of attention given to published works of primary materials and memoirs and published secondary sources at the expense of unpublished collections—despite the impressive bibliography suggesting extensive use of the latter. Firsthand accounts in the Manuscript Division of the Library of Congress, the Virginia Historical Society, the U.S. Army Military History Institute, the Southern Historical Collection at the University of North Carolina, Chapel Hill, George Mason University, the Richmond Battlefield Park, the Petersburg National Battlefield Park, and the William Perkins Library at Duke University are listed in an impressive compilation of sources, but are scarcely cited in the footnotes. Maney claims that he researched newspapers from Richmond, Philadelphia, New York, and Washington, but this reviewer could find but two footnote references, both to New York newspapers. He also may be unfamiliar with *The Civil War Memoirs of Captain William J. Seymour* (1991), edited by my colleague Terry L. Jones, a valuable account that covers most of the period, although he quotes Seymour from Jones' own monograph entitled *Lee's Tigers*. In brief, his footnotes and bibliography do not seem to be completely compatible. Another problem with this book is the maps. With one exception all those depicting the battlefield are useless. The author would have been better served if he had drawn his own maps, removed some of the darker background coloration, and cut down on the amount of information printed onto each plate. Quite useful, however, is his appendix, which includes an organizational chart for both armies at Cold Harbor on June 1, 1864.

In spite of this reviewer's criticism of some aspects of this monograph, Maney has managed to assimilate published primary and secondary materials as well as unpublished manuscript collections into a single volume, all of which should prove quite useful to those Civil War historians, buffs, and reenactors interested in this narrow study. Indeed, more research remains to be done during the war's final years, as evidenced by Maney's concentration on this brief period in 1864 leading to Cold Harbor. Such studies in microcosm allow for better synthesis to evolve, especially in the latter stages of the war.

Marshall Scott   Legan Northeast Louisiana University

Morning at Willoughby Run, July 1, 1863, by Richard S. Shue (Thomas Publications, 353 Buford Ave., Gettysburg, PA 17325), 1995. Photos, notes, biblio. 321pp. Paper. $19.95.

In *Morning at Willoughby Run*, Richard Shue has captured the dramatic opening events of the Battle of Gettysburg in great detail, though with more concentration on the Union side of the story. Shue begins by describing how the armies came together on the hills and valleys west of the town on July 1, 1863, before carrying the narrative to the point where a distinct lull in the fighting occurred around noon that day, where he essentially concludes his study. Two additional chapters provide an assessment of the morning's fighting and commentary on some "controversial" points about the battle.

Shue includes a vast number of quotations, allowing the actors to speak for themselves, and this is one of the book's stronger points. In the end, however, it is Shue's intervening commentary, the glue that binds those quotations to a readable narrative, that sometimes fails to hold the work together. Shue's prose is of distinctly uneven quality. Although some of his comments are merely inane, others are illustrative of more serious misinterpretations or shallow analyses. An example of the latter may be found in a brief portion of the book describing the initial call for Federal militia in Pennsylvania to counter the Confederate threat to the state. Response was poor, but Shue fails to comment on why that was so. The Stanton-instigated novelty of a militia controlled by the Federal government, with no definite term of service prescribed, no bounty, and the uncertainty of payment in general, all led Pennsylvanians to look askance at such a scheme. Notwithstanding the Keystone state's providing the Army of the Potomac with a total number of regiments and batteries larger than that of any other state, Shue concludes his brief discussion of the recruiting efforts with the startling comment that "Patriotism, evidently, was not a strong virtue among Pennsylvanians in the 1860s" (p. 9). This seems to be a flippant dismissal of a complex issue.

There are a number of additional problems that render the book suspect. Thus, as a popular history it is only passable; as a work of scholarship it is seriously flawed. Despite Shue's opening commentary about the care that must be exercised in evaluating the memoirs of participants (p. ix), he seemingly throws such caution to the wind early in the work. On page three, for example, readers will find a quote about the sagacity of Robert E. Lee's decision to invade Pennsylvania from the one person who epitomizes the need for a careful evaluation of underlying motives, Jubal Early. The quoted remark is taken from an article that appeared in the *Southern Historical Society Papers* while Early was its president. As one of the primary defenders of the Lost Cause and an influential proponent of Lee as the symbol of that cause, Early could be expected to say little else about Lee's decision. Unfortunately, owing largely to the limited types of source materials consulted, Shue continues to disregard his own admonition throughout the book. Reference to manuscript collections are regretfully scarce, and he relies continually on primary source material written by participants long after the din of battle faded to a distant memory. Their purple prose is reproduced at face value far too frequently throughout a book that purports to clarify many of the battle's controversies and misunderstandings.

All of this is not to say that Shue's book is not backed by significant research. Rather, he seems to be of the opinion that there is some direct correlation between the number of footnotes in a book and its excellence of scholarship. In this case there is not, and Shue goes overboard by footnoting excessively in what could be termed a misguided attempt to establish credibility. On page three is a paragraph containing five brief sentences that include biographical information on Maj. Gen. John F. Reynolds. Each sentence is footnoted! Yet, no sources are cited for several direct quotations appearing later in the text. In still other places, information that rightly belongs in the text is contained in lengthy footnotes that only serve to interrupt the flow of a good story.

Oddly enough, hand-in-hand with the earlier criticism of Shue's ready acceptance of possibly biased accounts is the fact that when he does apply his own critical analysis to those accounts, he is sometimes overly harsh. For example, he accuses Col. Edward B. Fowler of the 84th New York (Fourteenth Brooklyn) of making "misleading" statements in his official report about the 6th Wisconsin advancing to his regiment's assistance (p. 286). Since Fowler's regiment, along with the 95th New York, already had been engaged heavily and were in the process of changing front to meet a threat to their flank along the Chambersburg Pike, the advance of the Wisconsin regiment to the Pike could rightly be construed as its coming to the aid of the New Yorkers, not vice-versa as Shue contends. In addition, Fowler is as much as labeled a liar for stating that he ordered a charge on the Confederates in the railroad cut north of the pike and for his assertion that he also ordered the 6th Wisconsin to advance and flank the cut. Shue's criticism is based solely on a statement contained in Col. Rufus R. Dawes' memoirs of his service as commander of the 6th Wisconsin, in which Dawes denied receiving orders from Fowler and claimed not to have known that he was even on the field until after the battle. The possibility is not even mentioned that, in the confusion of battle, both men could have been correct. Furthermore, the reason for dismissing Fowler's statements as misleading on the sole basis of Dawes' denial is not clear. Such episodes, though minor, seem to call into question Shue's evaluative judgments. Other instances of faulty reasoning and what seems to be carelessness could be cited. For example, the author's use of Col. Charles S. Wainwright's official report as the source of information about Brig. Gen. James S. Wadsworth riding to Wainwright, requesting the use of his batteries, and being denied, is suspect. "Wainwright bluntly refused. Too hazardous the artillery chief said" (p. 167). Perhaps he did say so, but nowhere in his report is such an exchange mentioned.

In his efforts to evaluate some of the controversies surrounding the morning's action, Shue selects events that, though interesting, have little historical significance. His greatest mistake is in trying to make definitive conclusions about muddled events that have been further obfuscated by discrepancies between existing accounts. One could make an educated historical guess based on careful analysis of those accounts, but it is unlikely that many of them can be resolved conclusively. Even if they could be resolved, do we really need to know who fired the first shot of the Battle? Such information seems better suited for a book on Gettysburg trivia. Couple all of the previous complaints with oddly-turned phrases and the use of words such as "furtherest" (p. 57), and one may begin to have an idea of the extent of the problems plaguing this work.

Sadly, Shue's book adds little to our understanding of the events that unfolded on the morning of July 1, 1863. Readers would be better served by reading standard works, such as Edwin B. Coddington's *The Gettysburg Campaign: A Study in Command*, among others.

Edward J. Hagerty   American Military University

Unspoiled Heart: The Journal of Charles Mattocks of the 17th Maine, edited by Philip N. Racine (University of Tennessee Press, Knoxville, TN 37996-0325), 1994. Maps, illus., endnotes, index, d.j., 446pp. Cloth. $36.00

The 17th Maine was mustered into service in August 1862, and for a brief time participated in the defense of Washington, D.C. That relatively safe duty was short lived, however, and soon thereafter the 17th found itself at the front with the Army of the Potomac, first in the 3rd Corps and during the latter part of the war with the 2nd Corps. The regiment was active at Fredericksburg, Chancellorsville, Gettysburg, the "Overland Campaign," the siege of Petersburg, and the Appomattox Campaign. In the process it lost 370 men, nearly half of them to disease.

Unspoiled Heart is the wartime journal of Charles P. Mattocks, an officer in the 17th Maine. He was a well-educated, twenty-two-year-old who rose from the rank of lieutenant to major during his time in service. Descended from an old Massachusetts family that settled in the New World during the seventeenth century, Mattocks was the quintessential, strait laced New England gentleman. He was a graduate of Bowdoin College, located in Brunswick, Maine, and one of his instructors was Professor Joshua Chamberlain.

After eight months in the service, Mattocks began to write a detailed journal which he kept up until the end of the war. Mattocks' writings cover combat, campaigns, and daily camp life. He was captured at the Wilderness in early May 1864, and thereafter kept a detailed commentary on prison life.

Many Civil War diaries are mundane and uninspired. Mattocks', however, was not only well educated but a careful observer of events and a good writer. His accounts of the fighting at Chancellorsville, Gettysburg and the Wilderness are vivid, and augmented with maps that Mattocks drew depicting battle sectors in which his regiment was involved.

Mattocks' account of the Gettysburg campaign is particularly interesting and filled with anecdotes describing the towns, civilians, and incidents on the march to and from that great battle. On the march to Pennsylvania he noted that many of his men needed shoes and that some were barefoot. During the retreat from Gettysburg he provided observations of Sharpsburg and Harpers Ferry, where the Army of the Potomac had fought the previous year. After inspecting Lee's abandoned earthworks around Williamsport, he added weight to the claim that these were formidable works indeed.

In the spring of 1864, Major Mattocks was put in command of the 1st United States Sharpshooters. This famous unit had fallen on hard times and suffered both from attrition and lack of discipline. A skeptical Mattocks noted "I took out the invincible Sharp Shooters for the first time. We did fairly. They are clothed in every shape (some of them), and present anything but a martial appearance. By stupendous and untiring efforts I propose to soon get them to look better." In a later entry he stated, "These fellows are very proficient in the skirmish drill, but that is all they are good for." Nonetheless, after witnessing their marksmanship during the attack and capture of a Confederate redoubt, he gained respect for their prowess in combat.

After his capture at the Wilderness, Mattocks was shuffled around to a number of Southern prisons. His descriptions of life in captivity are among the most detailed to be found in any Civil War account. He finally escaped from his South Carolina prison and made it to the Smokey Mountains of western North Carolina, where he was aided by many locals who were Union sympathizers. This section of his journal alone is worth the price of the book for its descriptions of life in the mountains during the war. Before they could make it to the safety of Unionist East Tennessee, the young major and his party were captured by Confederate Cherokees of the Thomas Legion. Mattocks returned to prison but was exchanged in February 1865.

By April 1865 Mattocks was back at the front with the 17th Maine. He provides a graphic depiction of the final days of the war in Virginia, and at Saylor's Creek he led a charge which earned him the Medal of Honor.

This is one of the best written and most interesting accounts I have ever read. It will appeal to a wide audience and is an essential volume for students of the Chancellorsville and Gettysburg campaigns, prison life, life in nineteenth century Appalachia, and army life in general. Indeed this work provides a microcosmic look at many sub-themes of both military and social history.

Ted Alexander   Historian, Antietam National Battlefield

Blood & Treasure: Confederate Empire in the Southwest, by Donald S. Frazier (Texas A & M University Press, Drawer C, College Station, TX 77843-4354), 1994. Photos, notes, Biblio., d.j. 343pp. Cloth. $29.95

The primary premise of Donald Frazier's *Blood & Treasure* is that widespread Southern desire for the expansion of its slave empire motivated the Confederate invasion of the Southwest in 1861. He supports this thesis with the contention that the South required territory for the expansion of its society.

The first two chapters describe the historical context of a growing if fragmented regional desire for slave expansion into the Southwest and Spanish-speaking America. The fruits of the Mexican-American War and the Gadsen Purchase intensified the growing, bitter inter-sectional struggles about the role of slavery and its place in the Union. The author credits the Knights of the

Golden Circle (KGC) with materially aiding and abetting the dream of Southern expansion. He gives historical credence of the Knights' significance through an examination of the continual efforts by Texas to conquer territory in both Mexico and its New Mexico possession before 1846.

Frazier reemphasizes the crucial role played by the Knights. First, the activities of the KGC flamed sectional desire and commitment to slave expansion. Second, the organization linked expansion with conquest. Third, with the movement primarily based in Texas by 1860, the membership of the Texas Castles were a tremendous asset in capturing Federal personnel, fortifications, and provisions in Texas during the early months of 1861. Fourth, the aims of the organization logically linked Texas and Southern desires for expansion into the Southwest with Confederate military and political aims. Finally, many Texas Knights participated in the Confederate expedition.

Chapters three to six narrate the beginning of the Confederate invasion into the West, and Frazier's interpretation gives way to a chronology about people, places, and events. Confederate John Robert Baylor secured the Rio Grande valley above El Paso, organized as its governor the Confederate Territory of Arizona, threw a column west toward Tucson, and attempted to suppress the Apaches. A brief skirmish at San Tomas, the defense of Mesilla against Maj. Isaac Lynde and several battalions of Federal Regulars, and the Southern pursuit and capture of Lynde's force at San Augustin Springs, secured Confederate Arizona.

Colonel Baylor's emotional instability and concern about personal grandeur rapidly undermined his effectiveness. The governor's political appeasement of Hispanics gained him the enmity of the Anglo—Celtic population. His shooting and killing of editor Robert Kelly in December 1861, from which Baylor escaped through his manipulation of the martial law he controlled, foreshadowed coming Confederate difficulties. The arrival of Brig. Gen. Henry Hopkins Sibley with his headquarters unit the day following Kelly's death marked Baylor's inevitable demise as a major player in the events of Confederate Arizona.

Chapters six through thirteen continue the saga of the Confederates in the West, from the dispatch of Sibley's Brigade in October 1861, to the retreat of its remnants to San Antonio the following summer and fall. The reader follows the trek of rank and file as the Texas units struggle across the arid country to the chimera of New Mexico, in the process becoming familiar with the personnel of the Second, Four, Fifth, and Seventh Texas Mounted Cavalry, the Arizona Battalion, the San Elizario Spy Company, Roy Bean's "Free Rovers" (also known as "the Forty Thieves"), and other units.

The author's narrative closely describes Sibley's military campaign in which two Texan victories at Valverde and Glorietta Pass come to naught. The

Texans proved to be superb warriors but poor soldiers. Confederate logistical inability in providing adequate rations and other military items for the men and animals continually and seriously afflicted the Southern war effort from start to finish.

While the Confederates held their own at Glorietta Pass and forced Canby's Federals from the field of battle, the capture of the Southern supply train by a Union mounted force effectively ended the South's campaign for empire. Growing Union strength and the Texans' inability to provide for themselves soon forced the Southern units to retreat to San Antonio, never to return.

The final chapter and Epilogue returns from the narrative/descriptive mode to the interpretative style that Frazier uses so well in the beginning of the work. The author concludes that the drive for a Southern empire failed in the West because of several factors. The Confederate campaign was a logistical nightmare, from the failure of providing adequate provisions for men and animals to medical supplies for the wounded and ill. Canby and other Federal officers, while not as tactically proficient as their Southern opponents, demonstrated a strategic comprehension and doggedness unmatched by Southern commanders. Ultimately the Texans were unable to maintain the discipline and routine required for a successful military campaign

Most of all, however, the two primary Confederate commanders failed. Sibley and Baylor were not fit for their jobs and were incompatible in design and operation. Sibley, with the good qualities normally associated with those of a competent staff officer, displayed neither tactical nor strategic adeptness; additionally, he suffered from kidney disease compounded by alcoholism. Baylor, a good planner and a brave man, proved to be a self-promoting schemer who destroyed his effectiveness as governor because of his inability to separate pride from position. Once Sibley shunted Baylor aside, the latter worked unceasingly against his superior.

Frazier correctly states that any Southern desire to establish a southwestern empire was delusional, not in its concept but in the Confederacy's inability to commit and sustain resources sufficient for success. The author notes that the Union would have committed the necessary troops and logistical support from the Pacific states and territories—and from the Upper Midwest—if the South had seized California, its ports, and gold supply. The North would have had no alternative but to use its preponderance of resources to crush any Southern expansion into California.

Blood & Treasure is competently researched. The author delves into primary work from various local, state, and national archives, and demonstrates proficiency in using the important secondary works pertaining to his project. His descriptive narration of the campaign includes a multitudinous series of observations from the Confederate participants who penned journals, diaries and memoirs about their experiences in the West. He and other historians of this era should acquaint themselves with the work of Linda Hudson, a doctoral student at the University of North Texas, about the Knights of the Golden Circle.

While well researched, Frazier's writing style is better suited to the professional historian and thus will likely prove difficult on occasion for the lay reader. He is at his best in the interpretative and descriptive modes. When creating a narrative history of military operations (the bulk of chapters three to thirteen), the author should have remembered most readers more easily comprehend troop movements through geographic description than through the observations of participants. This *caveat* does not detract from Frazier's demonstrated excellence in quoting primary sources to enhance the particular of individual reactions to the larger event. When quoting a participant, the author could improve audience comprehension by identifying the participant's troop unit and its position.

The technical quality of this work has some difficulties. For example, the lack of an index hinders the researcher and interested lay reader. A few typographical errors exist that may disturb the reader's attention, and poor reproductions mar some of the illustrations.

While the campaigns of Baylor and Sibley were exercises in futility, this work is not. Not withstanding some of the problems mentioned above, Donald Frazier's *Blood & Treasure: Confederate Empire in the Southwest,* adds to the history of this Civil War period. His analysis seems solid. The book is a worthwhile if not definitive addition for historians and laymen alike interested in the topic.

Melvin C. Johnson   Texas Forestry Museum

To the Manner Born: The Life of General William H. T. Walker, by Russell K. Brown (University of Georgia (Athens) Press), 1994. Preface, photos, maps, appendix, notes, biblio., d.j. 411pp. Cloth. $50.00.

William Henry Talbot Walker is not a Civil War general many people can identify. Indeed, only serious students of the war may recognize his name and remember that he died in the fierce fighting near Atlanta in the summer of 1864. Walker had all the prerequisites to be a great fighting general, but he had a quarrelsome nature that prohibited him from achieving that ambition. In this fine biography, Russell K. Brown has described a man whose self-defeating personality relegated him to the shadows, a Confederate general that history has overlooked.

Born in Augusta, Georgia, in 1816, Walker graduated from West Point in 1837 and received praise for his service in both the Mexican and Seminole wars. But nothing ever pleased Walker, and his mood swings made him difficult, even on his best days. The author suggests that part of the trouble stemmed from the medicine that Walker took to ease the pain from old war wounds, three suffered in Florida and one in Mexico. Added to his chronic asthma, Walker was never a healthy man. Devoting one-third of the book to Walker's prewar career, the author depicts an ill, contentious individual quick to anger, a man at war with himself.

During the first two years of the Civil War, Walker was just another obscure soldier. He had gone to Virginia to offer his services to the Confederacy, but resigned in October 1861 and returned home where he assumed command of Georgia State Troops. He did not return to the Confederate Army until 1863, when he took a brigade to Vicksburg. Although promoted to major general while in Mississippi, the author concludes, "this may have been as much a comment on the lack of credentials of the other brigade commanders as it was on Walker's talents" (p. 288). Walker hoped to distinguish himself in action at the September 1863 Battle of Chickamauga. Instead, politics within the army and Walker's truculent nature kept him from achieving that goal. He watched others lead his men as his regiments, relegated to the reserves, were committed to the action piecemeal. Nonetheless, placing Walker in a secondary combat role failed to stop him from bluntly voicing his opinion concerning affairs within the army's high command.

When Maj. Gen. Patrick R. Cleburne proposed emancipating slaves, Walker was furious. Granted an extended leave of absence from the U.S. Army in 1856 because of bad health, Walker had returned home to become part of the South's planter class, and owned 100 slaves himself. He claimed that the proposal to arm slaves went against "all the teachings of my youth and the mature sentiments of my manhood" (p. 197). In spite of Gen. Joseph E. Johnston's desire to downplay Cleburne's paper, Walker forwarded the controversial proposal to President Jefferson Davis.

Walker was killed later that year in the Battle of Atlanta on July 22, 1864. An illtempered, volatile hothead, Walker was frustrated by events and personalities from gaining glory and honor in the army. He might have been a great Civil War general who students of the war would study with all the seriousness awarded other accomplished Confederate commanders. Instead, he died almost unknown.

This is a well-documented and comprehensive biography of a complex personality. Brown has done an excellent job of remaining unbiased, trying to see Walker as others saw him. Walker will never be considered a major player in the great drama of the Civil War. Nevertheless, this is a useful and interesting contribution to the growing literature of neglected Civil War figures.

Anne J. Bailey   University of Arkansas

Southern Railroad Man: Conductor N. J. Bell's Recollections of the Civil War Era, edited by James A. Ward (DeKalb: Northern Illinois University Press), 1994. Illus., notes, index, 194pp. Cloth. Contact publisher for price.

Nimrod J. Bell published *Railroad Recollections for over Thirty-Eight Years* in a limited edition in 1896. It passed quickly into obscurity and remained unknown until nearly a century. James A. Ward rescued Bell's narrative and has presented it to the public in an attractive and readable form. Ward's introduction provides a succinct portrait of the duties and responsibilities of a railroad conductor as well as an overview of Bell's life. The first eleven chapters present a chronological story of Bell's activities, while the last four treat various topics.

Bell's memoirs are important because he describes railroading from the perspective of a laborer and because his story deals with Southern railroads during one of the most critical periods of American history. According to Ward, "Bell tells us as much about the social and cultural mores of his homeland as he does about the complexities of operating trains across hundreds of miles of Southern rural America" (p. vii).

Born in South Carolina in 1830, Bell decided early in his life that he wanted to work for a railroad. He was married and trying to support four children when the Civil War began, but Confederate authorities exempted railroad men from the draft. Bell expressed satisfaction with this: "I was not mad enough to fight, and I always had to be awful mad to fight any way" (p. 10). He worked first on the Western & Atlantic between Chattanooga, Tennessee, and Atlanta, Georgia. Later he joined the East Tennessee & Georgia, which connected Knoxville, Tennessee, and Dalton, Georgia. Bell remained with this line until the end of the war. In his narrative, he provided vivid descriptions of accidents and problems caused by the troops, including some Louisiana soldiers who knocked several of their comrades off the train.

The Union occupation of Knoxville disrupted the East Tennessee & Georgia. In December 1863, Bell made his way from eastern Tennessee through Virginia and the Carolinas to Augusta, Georgia. He then operated trains on several lines running into the Carolinas. Among the unusual situations he encountered during the latter part of the war was the abandonment of several trains by their engineers in Wilmington, North Carolina, because they found it more profitable to participate in the lucrative blockade running at that port than in railroading. Bell, like other Southerners, welcomed the end of the conflict in the Spring of 1865. He stated that he had prayed at first for the Confederacy to succeed but later "prayed for the close of the war any way—just so as to stop it, and that we might have peace once more in our country" (p. 33).

Bell's railroading days continued through the bleak years of Radical Reconstruction and into the latter years of the century. He worked for the Alabama & Chattanooga, 1868-1877; South & North Railroad of Alabama, 1871-1872; Alabama & Chattanooga, 1872-1876; and East Tennessee, Virginia & Georgia, 1876-1895. Six of his chronological and all four of his topical chapters describe these years. An accident cut short Bell's career, and he disappears from the historical record after the publication of his recollections.

As the editor points out in his introduction, the conductor held an extremely important position in the workings of nineteenth century railroads. Bell had supervision over other employees on the train, had to make sure the train maintained its schedule, and was responsible for attaching and detaching the proper cars at the correct locations. He hired many of the employees he supervised and tried to make sure the engineer and fireman worked together smoothly. When he was on a passenger train, Bell was responsible for checking tickets, handling passengers' complaints, cleaning the cars, and supervising the sleeping cars.

The reader not only learns how Bell handled these varied tasks from day to day, but also some of the social mores of the nineteenth century. Bell expressed the prejudices typical of that time regarding women, blacks, Jews, and Orientals. Finally, the reader gains some insight into the unionization of railroad workers, a movement that led ultimately to "powerful railroad brotherhoods" (p. xxi).

Civil War scholars and buffs, however, will be disappointed to a degree with this book. Only twenty or so pages cover the war years, and these contain largely anecdotal material rather than anything of lasting historical significance. Additionally, editor Ward's Civil War "expert" did not serve him well. Ward states that this person "verified the book's wartime chronology" and also "looked up references. . .to obscure Southern generals" (p. ix).

Unfortunately, there are errors of both chronology and identification in Ward's notes. In several places, Bell discussed transporting Gen. Braxton Bragg's army from Knoxville to Chattanooga. A note speculates incorrectly that this occurred in 1863, even though Bell stated that the Confederates were returning from the invasion of Kentucky (late 1862). Similarly, Bell mentioned Bragg's army being at Tullahoma, Tennessee. The note to the statement says that this was in 1862, even though the army's occupation of that town was during the following year.

Several misidentifications of Confederate officers and units mar the explanatory notes. Prominent Tennessean and general Benjamin Franklin Cheatham is given the middle initial "E." Another note identifies a General Vaughan who had his headquarters at Loudon, Tennessee, as Alfred J. Vaughan. The latter was actually with his troops on Missionary Ridge, while Brig. Gen. John C. Vaughan led a cavalry brigade located at Loudon. Another note states that a General Wright "probably was General Marcus J. Wright" when the person could have been no one else. Finally, a Colonel Carter and his regiment at Charleston, Tennessee, go unidentified. The *Official Records* show this to have been Col. John Carpenter Carter and his 38th Tennessee Regiment, detached from Marcus Wright's Brigade to garrison the Tennessee town when the brigade moved to Missionary Ridge in November 1863.

This reviewer has some concern about Ward's treatment of "Gen. Forrest," who Bell said tried after the war to get aid from the Alabama legislature for a railroad for which he worked. The note to Bell's account states that Forrest "was reputed to have ordered the slaughter of several hundred African-American soldiers. . .at Fort Pillow" (p. 187). Rather than identifying Forrest as the president of the Selma, Marion & Memphis Railroad (1868-1874) and saying that his cavalry troopers had specialized in destroying railroads during the war, Ward brings up a charge that recent scholarship has shown to be totally untrue. Forrest issued no such orders and personally stopped some of his soldiers from shooting black soldiers who fell into Confederate hands.

The notes to this book are not as informative as they might have been. No sources are given in any notes except those for the introduction. There are no notes on the murder of the sheriff of Hamilton County, Tennessee, and his deputy by brothers releasing a third brother from custody. Bell gave the incident fairly prominent coverage—seven pages of text—and dates it in September 1882. Newspapers and court documents probably would have revealed details on the incident if they had been consulted. Likewise, there are no notes on the accidental death of a young man that was blamed on Bell. Bell quoted a newspaper account, but it is not cited.

Despite these shortcomings, readers will enjoy Bell's recollections. His story is well written and tells us much "about the complexities of operating trains across hundreds of miles of Southern rural America" (p. vii).

Arthur W. Bergeron, Jr.   Louisiana Office of State Parks

Far, Far From Home, by Guy R. Everson & Edward H. Simpson, Jr. (Oxford University Press, 200 Madison Ave., New York, NY 10016), 1994. Photos, index. 315pp. Paper. $14.95.

The Civil War letters of Richard "Dick" Wright and Taliaferro "Tally" Simpson of Pendleton, a rural town in the South Carolina upcountry, contain humorous anecdotes, romantic intrigue, and tragic events. Covering the period from the beginning of the war to the Battle of Chickamauga, these letters not only capture the vicissitudes of Dick and Tally, but also provide a look at their family on the home front. Life behind the lines for the Simpsons was not unlike that of tens of thousands of Southern families disrupted by the war. From these pages a clear picture emerges of the military experiences of two ordinary soldiers in the Confederate army. Intelligent and conscientious, the young men wrote poignantly about their happiness and frustrations, their triumphs and defeats.

In April 1861, Dick, a 20-year-old, and Tally, nearly two years older, left Wofford College in Spartanburg to join a company of the 3rd South Carolina Volunteers. The sons of Richard Franklin and Mary Margaret Simpson, their father was a signer of the Ordinance of Secession that paved the way for South Carolina to secede from the United States on December 20, 1860. According to Tally, the aforementioned date was "sacred" to his unit and would "be remembered by future generations" as the day the Palmetto State separated "from a detestable Union" (p. 100).

Motivated by Southern nationalism, the Pendleton natives believed that it was their obligation to join the Confederate cause. In a letter to his mother written two days after the attack on Fort Sumter, Dick wrote, "This is no rash act, but my feeling of duty urges me to it" (p. 4). The two enlisted men represented a martial spirit that was common to the South during the antebellum period.

The young soldiers' letters reveal their confidence in and devotion to the Confederate States of America. Patriotic enthusiasm did not make it any easier for them to endure the hardships of camp life or to cope with loneliness. They reminisced about growing up at Mt. Jolly, the family homestead, and looked forward to returning to enjoy the luxuries of home. Constant drilling, combined with long hours of marching caused many soldiers to collapse from physical exhaustion. Sleeping on wet blankets and the bloodthirsty insects in search of a feast added to the soldiers' discomfort. The wartime letters of Dick and Tally make several references to the poor quality of food, which often consisted of rank bacon, stale bread, and cold mutton, and their attempts to supplement their diet by purchasing rations whenever possible.

Letters were cherished items in a soldier's life, and Tally never hesitated to admonish family members for not writing. Not only did he appreciate numerous letters, but lengthy ones as well. To be kept informed about family matters on the home front helped him to deal with the monotony associated with military life. On the romantic side, Tally displayed youthful exuberance during his flirtatious involvement with Fannie Smith of Pendleton, but their relationship never developed beyond the infatuation stage because of Tally's untimely death.

The Simpson brothers often commented on the death of comrades, which served as a vivid reminder to them that perishing in battle or succumbing to disease was a reality of war. Dick's affiliation with the Confederate army ended in July 1862, when he was discharged because of illness. This explains why most of the letters in this volume were written by Tally. In fact, of the 120 letters in this book, ninety were penned by him. After the war, Dick practiced law, served in the South Carolina legislature, and chaired the board of trustees of Clemson College.

Tally, in providing details on military operations, included analysis of the battles in which he participated. Illustrative of this was his observation following the Confederate victory at Bull Run in July 1861. Writing to his sister Mary on August 1, Tally said, "Just after their defeat we could easily have gone and taken possession of Washington without the least difficulty" (p. 38). Tally saw action in most the major battles in the Eastern Theater, including First Manassas, Seven Pines, Second Manassas, Antietam, Fredericksburg (where hewas wounded), Chancellorsville, and Gettysburg. Tally, however, had a penchant for exaggerating the strength of the enemy. In a letter to his sister Anna on September 24, he claimed that George B. McClellan's army at Sharpsburg numbered more than 200,000 troops. In actuality, the Union force there was less than half that amount. Tally found reprehensible the pillaging of civilian property by Confederate soldiers. It is somewhat perplexing that Corporal Tally, with his ambition, educational background, and political connections, never advanced beyond that low rank.

A few weeks after the Battle of Gettysburg, James Longstreet's First Corps which included the 3rd South Carolina, was ordered to the Western Theater to assist Braxton Bragg. By then, Tally had become a mature veteran tested under fire in several hard fought battles in the East. Tally's life came to a tragic end on Georgia soil, as he was killed at the Battle of Chickamauga on September 20, 1863, "far, far from home." The last seven letters in this volume are expressions of sympathy to Tally's loved ones following his death. The proud South Carolinian was remembered as a courageous soldier who became a casualty of war while facing the enemy. He was laid to rest in the small Simpson family cemetery in his home town. Dick, who died in 1912, was interred near his brother. In death as in life, they were side by side.

The editors place each chapter of letters in historical context with an introductory statement on the general theme therein. Their use of explanatory footnotes to identify individuals, places, or to correct errors made by Dick and Tally add a dimension of clarity to this work. This book also contains a short bibliography, a chronology of the letters—including the place from which each was written, and a listing of the "cast of characters" which helps to identify members of the Simpson family.

The epilogue chronicles the postwar careers and activities of the leading members of the Simpson family. With the exception of minor editorial changes, this collection of letters appears as originally written by the brothers. Illustrated with photographs, this volume enriches the historiography of the Civil War. The editors should be commended for their fine collaborative effort.

Leonne M. Hudson   Kent State University

Gettysburg: A Meditation on War and Values, by Kent Gramm (Indiana University Press, Bloomington, Indiana), 1994. Map, Note on sources, index. 270pp. Cloth. $24.95

There has never before been a book quite like this one on the Battle of Gettysburg, or for that matter such a book on any other battle of the American Civil War. Kent Gramm, novelist, has given us what appears in the Table of Contents as a standard treatment of the battle (The Peach Orchard, The Wheat-field, Pickett's Charge, etc.), but the contents are anything but standard. This work is essentially a book about values—those of the Civil War generation and our own—with a persistent emphasis upon character and courage, placed within an attempt to find the meaning of the Civil War and to find ourselves as well. The writing style itself will be jolting to many—an almost poetic voice that strives to attain the impact of Walt Whitman or Gramm's beloved Henry David Thoreau. Of works on Civil War battles, only portions of Jack McLaughlin's *Gettysburg: The Long Encampment* come closest to Gramm's thoughtful and often beautiful prose.

But to be forthright about this work, it must be underscored that many parts are irritating, seemingly ridiculous, or jarringly incongruous. For example, Gramm makes this observation on commercialism in modern day Gettysburg: "The flashier individuals—politicians and movie stars—make the tabloids, but the gas chambers of the nation's soul are places with nice lawns and central air" (p. 168). This is a work which manages to bring in Desert Storm, K-Mart, religious fundamentalists, Dan Quayle, Toys 'R Us, Shirley MacLaine, and a host of other random terms and names, and hurl them at us.

A sampling of such disparate views may serve to give a sense of what I mean, even with its danger of taking quotes out of context: ". . .but in 1980 all America became an actor, playing a part to deceive ourselves. Like locusts, like an undisciplined and demoralized army invading our own soil, we said, 'To hell with everything and everybody including our children, let's get some money.' And hey. Everything's O.K." (p. 76); "America is a geriatric debauchee rolling downhill in a Japanese wheelchair. We knew it in 1980, but we thought a patriot was someone who says, 'Let's forget the bad things and live as though nothing's wrong'" (p. 107); "I believe there is an America, but it is dead on the field. I hope it is not too late for some hand to pass across it: for the bones to rustle, knit together, stagger into flesh and close up in a battle line behind that earlier flag" (p. 160); "The South without its racism, the North without most everything but its ideals—now that would have been a Union worthy of the War. But what came out was the very opposite, a triumphant industrial state on its way to commercial totalitarianism, with a hardened, practical indifference to an unfree underclass" (p. 184).

I agree with Kent Gramm on many of these points, but he has presented them in an unsophisticated manner that will beckon to many simply because of the style in which it is written, in some parts akin to free verse in a prose format: "The ship of liberty—even the world of politics itself—floats like a ship upon the moral sea, which answers not to human pilots but to a distant moon and sun" (p. 258); "As they are, Iverson's men, so is Earth, betrayed by its friends, ambushed by its enemies. Waste, death, emptiness; no grass left to go to, only the stars" (p. 93); "It may be that a music seldom heard drifts among the stars, sweet beyond all measure, grand and subtle, terrible and comforting; that even in our small events its soft incline plays out mysterious harmonies; that somehow all will yet come right—and that we have been paying the wrong piper" (p. 104).

Many years ago, in a review I read of Bruce Catton's *The Hallowed Ground*, the reviewer objected vehemently to the last line of the book, concerning Catton's beautiful portrait of the Army of the Potomac's final parade in Washington, D.C. at war's end, a parade that lasted into the night by candlelight: "Somewhere, far beyond the night, there would be a brighter and a stronger light." I thought then that the reviewer was a poor pedantic soul with no imagination to see the meaning of such a metaphor. Therefore, I should be cautious not to appear so unfeeling in the face of such a book as this one, but I contend that much of it is for effect only, full of style but with little substance concerning modern culture; it is a book the author most certainly wrote primarily for himself and perhaps family and friends. Thus, many parts of the book contain Gramm's account of his visits to the Gettysburg battlefield, of people he met there and of his thoughts and experiences on those occasions—this is personal work by one who obviously feels deeply about what he has written.

This book is, needless to say, not an authoritative tactical study of the battle, nor a narrative of the campaign from invasion to Robert E. Lee's retreat. It does touch, however, upon many points of the battle, some in detail.

I think that what the author was attempting was what Baritz accomplished in his excellent *Backfire*, a passionate account of the Vietnam War in the context of American cultural history. Gramm's book will not make us think of ourselves, as Baritz did; we will, instead, think only of. . .Gramm, and his unusual and personal attempt to reach America's soul by examining America's greatest military contest.

Having said all this, I still recommend the book. There is much chaff here, but the quality of the grain makes it worthwhile.

David P. Smith   Garland, Texas

BOOK NOTES

Libby Life: Experiences of a Prisoner of War in Richmond VA 1863-64, by F. F. Cavada (Heritage Books, Inc., 1540-E Pointer Ridge Pl., Suite #300, Bowie, MD, 20716), 1994. 232pp. Paper. $20.00, and *Camp and Prison Journal*, by Griffin Frost (Camp Pope Bookshop, P.O. Box 2232, Iowa City, IA, 52244), 1994. Index. 315pp. Cloth. $32.00.

F. F. Cavada states that he wrote his journal "not with the object of presenting a sensational picture of the military prisons of the Confederacy, but simply to while away the idle hours of a tedious and protracted captivity." While I enjoyed reading *Libby Life*, I am not certain that it increased my knowledge about Civil War prisons. I was also disappointed that this reprint edition did not contain biographical information about Cavada. Knowing something about the man would add to the appreciation of his experiences.

Still, I found *Libby Life* to be very readable and enjoyable even though it was written over one hundred years ago. Cavada's writing is philosophical, optimistic, and at times, humorous. I believe, however, that Cavada filtered his prison experience through optimistic eyes.

In contrast, Griffin Frost states in his preface in *Camp and Prison Journal* that he is submitting his journal to the public as a truthful account of his terrible experiences of imprisonment in Northern prisons. His journal was written in response to the revelations of the treatment and conditions of Northern prisoners in Southern prisons. He writes that the atrocities of the Southern prisons could not have exceeded those of the Northern prisons. Frost's experiences as recorded in his journal, however. do not seem to support his forthright statement about atrocities in Northern camps.

Camp and Prison Journal is exactly that, a journal. An edited edition with some highlights and notable incidents, eliminating many entries that do not really add any enlightenment to Frost's experiences, would perhaps have been more useful. The biographical information that was added about Frost and his journal, however, was helpful and interesting.

Both books reviewed here offer us a glimpse into the experiences of the men that fought and were held captive in our nation's Civil War.

Frank G. Prator   El Cajon, CA

Ploughshares Into Swords: Josiah Gorgas and Confederate Ordnance, by Frank E. Vandiver (Texas A&M University: College Station), 1994. Preface, biblio., index. 349pp. $35.00

In the fall of 1958 the then Rice Institute took me in as a graduate student and Frank Everson Vandiver, still basking in the success of *Mighty Stonewall*, took on one of the earliest of his legion of graduate students to tutor in the arts of writing and speaking the history of the Civil War. I had read Vandiver's biography of Gen. Thomas J. Jackson the summer before, and everything he has written since, except, inexplicably, his first biography on Josiah Gorgas. Although I should have read it sooner, I am glad I waited. Reading it now as a former graduate student, friend, thirty-seven year admirer, and veteran of the academic experience, the measure at what was achieved by Vandiver in his twenties in this biography is even more impressive.

Vandiver the prodigy, who took this book as a "dissertation to Tulane in his suitcase," according to Wendell Holmes Stephenson, already possessed literary skills in 1952 that made this biography of Gorgas an example of the genre. It is a "life and times," for Vandiver goes into the details of Confederate logistics and administration along with those of his subject with equal zeal and depth. The specifics of Gorgas' life may be summed thusly: Pennsylvania-born and West Point-educated, Gorgas spent his pre-Civil War career at various posts as ordnance officer, mostly in the South. There he married, and when the time of choosing sides approached, he joined friends in the Confederate service and headed the Ordnance Bureau, plus several others until spun off as separate agencies, in splendid fashion, before finishing his life as vice-chancellor at Swanee and in the presidency of the University of Alabama.

Gorgas' administration of his bureau, Vandiver points out, surpassed every other Confederate supply agency. Soldiers might be barefoot, hungry, clad in rags, forced to walk in the absence of other transportation, but they always had weapons and ammunition. That the South had few facilities for providing either at war's beginning did not deter Gorgas: he built the facilities, utilized captured equipment, sent agents to procure it in the North when still possible and especially in Europe later and then ran the blockade with them; anything, it seems, to work his miracles.

Vandiver's view is that Gorgas possessed specific qualities that made his miracle: the ability to select efficient and trustworthy assistants; adaptability, as the war changed circumstances; good health for most of the war that enabled him to work long hours; and keen administrative skills that focused on the "big picture" but never forgot the specifics that composed that big picture.

Sometimes the old books remind us that the story has been told about as well as it is going to be told. This is such a book.

Archie P. McDonald   Stephen F. Austin State University

The Real War Will Never Get in the Books, edited by Louis P. Masur (Oxford University Press, 200 Madision Ave., New York, NY 10016)1993. Photos, notes, index, 301pp. Cloth. $25.00.

To many people, the Civil War means immense battles and larger-than-life military leaders. Walt Whitman, on the other hand, viewed such a portrait of the Civil War as superficial and felt that it ignored the internal history of the war—what Whitman called the "real war." Whitman's real war was not the battles themselves, but the individual courage, fear, tragedy, and triumph experienced by the participants before, during, and after battle. In Whitman's opinion history would be better served by studying how the dangers and wounds of battle were faced, rather than how the battles were conducted militarily. Notwithstanding, Whitman predicted that his real war, "the seething hell and black infernal background of countless minor scenes and interiors. . .will never get in the books" (p. 281).

The purpose of this compilation, titled after Whitman's prediction, is not to get Whitman's real war into print; to Masur, Whitman's Civil War writings are those of a prominent American writer of the era composed during, not after, the war. Masur argues that while the Civil War was a written war, the literary aspects have been somewhat elusive. By presenting selected writings of fourteen nationally prominent authors of the Civil War era, Masur's purpose is to introduce the reader to what he terms the "literary Civil War."

Masur suggests that this work is different from other similar studies in that it concentrates on the letters, diaries, speeches, and essays of the authors of the day, rather than on works of fiction written during the period. Aside from Whitman, Masur, in 281 pages of text, has included selections from Henry Brooks Adams, Louisa May Alcott, Lydia Maria Child, John Esten Cooke, John William De Forest, Frederick Douglass, Ralph Waldo Emerson, Charlotte Forten, Nathaniel Hawthorne, Thomas Wentworth Higginson, Herman Melville, William Gilmore Simms, and Harriet Beecher Stowe. Presented alphabetically, each chapter is prefaced by a Civil War era photograph of the author whose writings are being presented, and a two-page biographical sketch. These concise biographical sketches greatly enhance this collection by providing insight and understanding of each author's state of mind at the time the selections were penned.

Ron Calkins   Little Rock, Arkansas

War of Another Kind: A Southern Community in the Great Rebellion, by Wayne K. Durrill (Oxford University Press, P.O. Box 36, Lavallette, NJ 08735-9985), 1994. Appendix, notes, biblio., index. 288pp. Paper. $14.95.

Wayne Durrill's study of Washington County, North Carolina, during the American Civil War is fascinating, provocative, and at times frustrating. His exhaustively researched analysis of this small segment of one state illustrates the process by which planters, during the Civil War, lost the political control that they had enjoyed prior to the war. According to Durrill, yeoman farmers, who for the preceding few decades seemingly had supported the planters, viewed the Civil War as a struggle over property and supported the Union cause in the hope of loosening planter control. The title of the book's final chapter, "The End of a Plantation Community," implies that the yeoman farmers were successful.

Durrill claims that planters controlled the county and resentment against them lay just below the surface. Historians have uncovered similar scenarios throughout the South during the antebellum era, and so the reader is not surprised by Durrill's description of social relations in Washington County. However, Durrill traces the actions of many specific individuals throughout the war to discover the role they played in this changing social and political climate, and therein lies the strength of this book. As in many areas of the South, Washington County planters in the 1850s became increasingly fearful of a national government that could limit the expansion of slavery and might attempt to abolish the institution. Yeoman farmers, on the other hand, were dismayed by the planters' willingness to destroy the government over the issue of slavery, and by midsummer of 1861 had gravitated to the Unionist position. Thereafter the two groups struggled for control in state and local elections, focusing particularly on the local militia. The strength of this book is the focus on individuals as they played their various roles in this scenario.

While many questions are left unanswered, Durrill's book is a welcome addition to Civil War scholarship. His painstaking analysis of these shifting patterns in one county during the war illustrates the shaky foundation of planter political control and suggests an important avenue for further inquiry.

Nancy Smith   Midgette Elon College

From Ball's Bluff to Gettysburg. . .and Beyond, edited by Gregory A. Coco (Thomas Publications, P.O. Box 3031, Gettysburg, PA, 17325), 1994. Contact publisher for price.

While at first glance *From Ball's Bluff to Gettysburg. . .and Beyond* appears to be just another collection of Civil War letters detailing the typical service of an infantryman, this impression is not correct. Private Roland E. Bowen of the 15th Massachusetts Volunteer Regiment, wrote home to his friends and family on a fairly consistent basis, and his precise depictions of events, coupled with a flair of cockiness, grab the reader's attention and encourage further exploration. Although Bowen's experiences paralleled those of most combat-hardened veterans, his narrative of battles like Balls Bluff and Gettysburg, as well as two experiences as a prisoner of war, are far from ordinary.

Bowen's manuscript was discovered among the files of the Gettysburg National Battlefield. Editor Gregory A. Coco tracked the remaining set of letters through Bowen's living descendants. The letters trace his military career from its commencement on July 30, 1861, until his discharge three years later. Bowen described the fighting at Ball's Bluff as "such terrible confusion, men running to and fro, other leaping into the river. The horrid forms of the dead. . .the groans of the wounded and the heart rendering crys that would go up from a hundred drowning lips. Heaven forbid that I may never again witness such a scene as this" (p. 39) Bowen and the 15th Massachusetts would see action at Seven Pines, the Seven Days, Antietam, Fredericksburg, and Gettysburg.

Coco has done an admirable job editing Bowen's three year collection of letters. His footnotes are informative without being cumbersome. Photographs of personalties and places mentioned in the letters enhance Bowen's narrative, as does the comprehensive index, which lists all names and places mentioned in the manuscripts.

Mitchell Yockelson   National Archives

INDEX

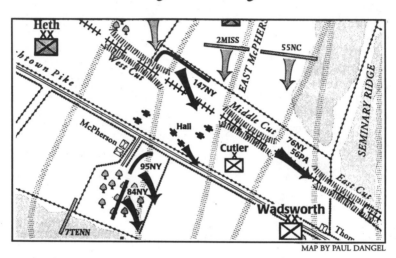